COMING TOGETHER—COMING APART

COMING TOGETHER—COMING APART

The Union of Opposites in Love Relationships

John Desteian

Plates III, VIII, X, XI, and XII from the *Splendor Solis* (London: Kegan
Paul, Trench, Trubner & Co. Ltd., N.D.) reprinted by permission of the
Yoga Publication Society, Homewood, IL

Pictures 1, 2, 3, and 9, drawn from the *Rosarium Philosophorum,* appear in
The Collected Works of C. G. Jung, volume 16, Bollingen Series XX,
copyright 1954, 1966 by Princeton University Press. Reprinted by permission.

Picture 6, The King in Bed, is drawn from Waite, A.E., *The Hermetic
Museum,* Volume One. Reprinted by permission of Samuel Weiser, Inc.,
York Beach, ME

SIGO Press
25 New Chardon Street, #8748
Boston, Massachusetts 02114

Publisher and General Editor: Sisa Sternback

International Standard Book Number: ISBN 0-938434-45-4 Cloth
ISBN 0-938434-44-6 Paperback

Library of Congress Cataloging-in-Publication Data:

Desteian, John A.
        Coming together/coming apart

        Bibliography: p.
        1. Love.   2. Marriage   3. Separation (Psychology)
I. Title
HQ801.D47   1989   306.7   88-15793.

To my wife, Judith

TABLE OF CONTENTS

LIST OF ILLUSTRATIONS

PREFACE

When do marital problems begin?

According to popular wisdom, troubles start as soon as the honeymoon is over. For some people this may refer to a period as short as a few months; for others, as long as two or three decades. The shorter the period, the more we are inclined to wonder why the couple married at all; alternatively, the longer the period the more we wonder what, after all these years, has induced them to separate. And when a marriage breaks up because one partner has fallen in love with another person, we may even blame the abandoned partner for failing to "hold" the wanderer.

At the same time, we often see lasting marriages that seem totally devoid of happiness, joy, mutual interests, or communication. Such couples are often seen in restaurants where they sit across the table from each other, scarcely speak, and then silently eat their food and depart. What, one wonders, keeps these couples together in what looks like an unrewarding and sterile parallel existence?

The proliferation of family therapists, marriage counselors, and divorce statistics confirm that many marriages are troubled. Unfortunately, many counselors take a band-aid approach to unhappy relationships, trying to alleviate symptoms rather than to explore why they came into existence. Among the helping professions, it is generally recognized that any therapeutic technique will be helpful to somebody,

if not necessarily everyone. Nevertheless, many counselors and therapists have the same advice for all clients:

> "You must learn to communicate better."
> "Tell her what you feel."
> "You must learn to trust."
> "You must learn to take risks."
> "You must be more open."

If the advice does not work, the fault is considered to lie in the clients
("they resisted the counselor") rather than in the nature of the advice.

In the course of my practice, I have learned that no matter how
carefully a psychological band-aid is applied or how skillfully a particular set of principles is drummed into a client, the relationship cannot
be reworked if all the counselor looks at is how the couple interact and
what feelings they express. Over and over again I have seen clients
who were on the verge of a divorce because, their counselors notwith-
standing, that seemed to be the only option open to them.

The complete diagnosis of a problematic marriage must start with
looking at the marriage not as a social institution or series of emotional
interactions, but rather as the culmination of a process that began when
the couple first met and became infatuated with each other. Why did
they fall in love with each other? What happened to their perceptions
of and feelings for each other after they married?

To answer these questions, we must explore the process of love and
marriage: how initial infatuation leads to marriage and then to the stage
at which many marriages seem first to lose their vigor and then to
become conflict-filled; then, why we are attracted to particular individuals, why others turn us off after a while, why temporary sexual alliances
excite us even if we recognize them as unsatisfactory, and why we are
drawn to inappropriate individuals; finally, why some marriages bring
growing fulfillment to the partners while others lead to growing distress.
I address the question of why some marriage partners seem to be totally
different from the persons with whom they fell in love, and of why
some partners find themselves behaving in ways that are alien to their
personalities. I shall use actual case histories to illustrate the points
(and problems) as they arise.

The ultimate goal of any marriage counseling is to infuse old marriages with new life. I shall show that in many relationships what seems
to be a lack of interest in the other is, in fact, a need to understand
more about oneself. At critical points in our lifetimes we disengage
from others and focus our attention on ourselves.

We can reanimate ourselves and our marriages. This process requires us to retrace our steps, this time with our accumulated knowledge, along the route from infatuation to marriage and onward to self-fulfillment.

John A. Desteian
St. Paul, Minnesota.

ACKNOWLEDGMENTS

I would like to thank Sylvia Rosen for teaching me any- and everything I may know about writing a book. If this work suffers as to style or content, the failure lies with the student, and not with the teacher. That Sylvia also edited the first half of this book is an added asset, and a further reason for my gratitude to her. I would also like to thank Marc Romano, whose wisdom and support have been instrumental in creating a work which is of readable length and quality. I would like to acknowledge the contributions of colleagues whose psychological wisdom has guided this work: Mario Jacoby, Neil Micklem, C.T. Frey. I would especially like to thank and gratefully acknowledge Martin Odermatt. I want to acknowledge the contributions of students and clients whose psychological material, interest and comments have challenged me to penetrate more deeply than I had ever imagined the mysteries of the psyche.

And finally, I would like to thank my son, who sacrificed time with his father so that this book could be finished; and my wife, Judith A. Savage, also a Jungian analyst, whose encouragement and psychological wisdom have helped to carry me back to my writing desk, even as I heard the quiet whispering of the golf course beckoning me.

CHAPTER I

INTRODUCTION

"How can I love someone that I can't live with?"

"I'm so sick of falling in love with women who are like injured birds. I always end up having to take care of them and my needs are never met."

"Whenever I fall in love I end up chasing my own tail. I feel like I have to do all the work. Then just when I make the commitment, she runs away."

"I love falling in love but I can't stand being around someone for very long. Once they have their hooks in you there's no getting away."

"There isn't a guy I've fallen in love with who didn't finally leave because, as they said, I was too much for them. They couldn't count on me to be there for them whenever they wanted me."

"I am always amazed that I become an insecure little boy whenever I fall in love. I'm better off by myself. At least then I'm not so dependent and weak."

These are some of the problems that have been bringing my group therapy clients to our weekly sessions for the past three or four years. At the core of their unhappiness is a pattern of failed heterosexual relationships. They fall in love easily and happily and glory in the elation and animation that infatuation brings, but when infatuation ends they discover again that the relationship is an unhappy one. After a few such experiences they begin to wonder why their love life is so unrewarding, and they wind up hoping to break the pattern by participat-

1

ing in one of the two therapy groups I conduct each week. They want, at first, answers to two questions:

"What makes me fall in love over and over again, even when I don't want to?"

"Why do I always fall in love with a particular kind of person?"

I have little difficulty answering the first question despite the puritanical attitude of our culture toward falling in love over and over again. How moralistic the media becomes when public figures openly live together or marry and divorce for the third, fourth, or even fifth time! But the extent of our need to know why can be measured by the popularity of advice columns and pop-psychology questionnaires. Too often we get pat answers: people need relationships; the intimacy of marriage prevents loneliness; marriage gives us companionship; we are better-adjusted people if we share our lives with someone.

However, whenever I am asked that first question, I simply respond that we fall in love because it is the natural thing for people to do, whether we are fifteen or fifty or seventy or ninety; we fall in love in order to become who and what we are.

Why we fall in love with a particular person, the second question, is more difficult to answer. In our youth we are told that we will "just know" who is right for us when the time comes; when we are mature we are told to let our brain, not our heart, pick the lover. But we all know that falling in love with a particular person has nothing to do with intelligence, and that often the individual who seems so right eventually turns out to be so wrong.

With experience, many of us gain some vague notions of the qualities we like in people. I say "vague" because it is not unusual for us to be attracted to partners who turn out to have few if any of those qualities. Or we recognize that we tend to fall in love with persons who remind us of or are totally unlike our opposite-sex parent. But even a man like "dear old Dad" or a young woman with all of Mom's qualities may not guarantee happiness. So after a few unhappy experiences we begin to wonder why we make such bad choices in lovers, and even whether something is wrong with us. If we try to get along without love, our life seems to have no joy until we find ourselves becoming enraptured again. We may even determine that this time we'll "make it work." For the participants in my therapy groups, that "this time" too often led to another cycle of unhappiness.

As a full-time analyst and part-time relationship counselor (I spend only four hours of my 40-hour work week engaged in group therapy), I am not there to tell the group participants what they are doing wrong or how to change their behaviors. To do the first would be to sit in judgment on them and to do the second would be to prescribe. Even if judging and prescribing were legitimate functions for counselors—and none of us is so all-knowing and wise that we can honestly engage in such activities—it would be a waste of time. It just doesn't do any good to tell someone, "Don't do that!" But there is also the fact that in order to make a judgment we have to understand first what a particular behavior means at a particular moment for a particular individual. One cannot generalize. The same behavior may have different significance not only for each person, but also for each person at different times. What is a positive trait in one experience is not necessarily positive in another.

In order for our love lives to match the fullness and richness of our potential for loving, we have to work from the inside out; that is, we have to start by understanding what within us is preventing us from achieving our goal. And even then we may repeat the destructive experience again and again until we finally get it into our heads that "This is what I need to do."

I like to think of myself in the group therapy sessions as taking on the role of an external mediator between the different parts of an individual's personality (I specify "external" because we all have a built-in internal mediator; I discuss this personality integrant in Chapter II). This role may mean asking the questions a participant is unable or reluctant to ask her/himself. For example, sometimes a participant turns to me after recounting a quarrel or some other hurtful experience and asks, "What did I do wrong?" However, I may see the problem as a conflict within the client. Thus, I turn the question around and ask, "What do you think you did wrong?" My intention is to encourage the client to bring the conflict to light and then I can step in to mediate between her or his needs and ego.

Sometimes a participant—let's say a male—will tell the group about how full of rage he has been all week, and that he knows he should not permit himself to behave in such a manner. I might ask about what inside him is so vulnerable that it needs rage as a protective device. The question is intended to relate his ego and the rage with which he has been living to the vulnerability. In other words, I would try to mediate between his vulnerability and his ego; my intention would be to help his ego integrate the vulnerability within his personality so he can find the necessary inner resources to heal the wounds inherent in that vulnerability.

Another example would be a woman who tells the group about a dream she has had of an Amazon, a tall, strong, powerful woman, who, in the dream, is able to clear all the physical obstacles in her path when she walks through the forest. Since the dreamer happens to be an unhappy, depressed, and weak person who often weeps and gives the impression of being inadequate, I see that dream image as having considerable value for her. I interpret it as another side of herself that is eager to be given life. My intention would be to mediate between the Amazon expressed in the dream and her conscious weak ego; I would hope that by helping her recognize the value of that strong and fearless part of herself, she would begin to integrate these traits within her conscious self-image.

At another time when a client asks, "What did I do wrong?" I may respond by asking a different question: "How do you think you betrayed yourself?" My purpose would not be to pass the buck but to encourage the client to look inward, to think in terms of how she behaved in a manner which was not in her self-interest.

The members of the therapy group do not just sit around listening to accounts of each other's experiences and what I hope will be my penetrating questions. In fact, I usually say very little during the session. What makes the group a therapeutic one is that, first, the clients are a community of peers with, in many respects, the same problems and goals. They quickly learn that their problems are neither unique nor shameful. Second, each brings an individual perception that adds a different dimension to the discussions and enriches them. Third, they form a strong support group for each other. They reinforce each participant's positive experiences and behaviors as well as his or her efforts to learn and to change. Fourth, and perhaps most important, they try to prevent each other from taking actions that are self-destructive or self-betraying.

The group's advice is not always welcomed. When group members insist, for example, "You can't permit yourself to do such and such!," "You can't permit yourself to call her or him!," "You can't loan him or her any more money!," or "You can't permit yourself to waver when you talk to him about X, Y, or Z!," the individual at the receiving end of the admonition often takes the stance that the group members are being hurtful, that they are trying to exert control over her or him, or that they are trying to limit her or his possible movements. In fact, however, the group is trying to prevent the individual from betraying her/himself (we all have a stake in betraying ourselves; we do it every time we "give in" to prevent an argument). And although it may take a while, the individual usually recognizes that fact, often even ruefully.

This book draws upon my experiences with members of current and past groups, but only as illustrations. I make no attempt here to counsel readers on problems. Specifically, this book has a theoretical rather than a clinical orientation, although the theory is amply illustrated with clinical materials. At group sessions I never talk about theory. When I interpret a client's behaviors, I may base what I have to say on a theoretical construct, but I do not discuss the construct itself. One reason is the danger of encouraging group participants to intellectualize their problems instead of seeking out their emotional roots. The latter is a painful process that takes considerable time whereas the former does not involve the emotions and can be used as a rationale to justify erratic and self-defeating behavior. Another reason is that the participants in the group meetings tend to be in crisis situations, that is, they are suffering; their wounds, however, are psychic rather than physical. If these clients were suffering from diseases, no medical practitioner would try to effect a cure simply by discussing the biological or physiological sources of illness and then explaining the theory of the treatment. Giving clients theoretical explanations of their problems does not cure them; it only expands their vocabularies. When Sigmund Freud first began practicing psychoanalysis in Vienna at the turn of the century, his method of treatment was dubbed "the talking cure"; today, "talking" is still the therapy of choice for patients with psychological problems.

Nevertheless, the kind of problems that are aired in my weekly groups were the seeds of my interest in affectional relationships. For the six years before I went to Zurich and studied to become a Jungian analyst, I worked with people who were on the verge of divorce or were engaged in legal suits as a result of divorce. After a while I realized that there was more to the post-divorce suits than the ostensible arguments over alimony, child support, or visitation rights. The suits, I came to understand, were a way of continuing the attachment with former partners, especially among couples who had been divorced for three or four years. After a while I saw a similarity between the post-divorce attachment and the initial infatuation: *the same kind of heat and passion operated in both states but in reverse*. When it came time to write the dissertation for my diploma from the Jung Institute, I thus chose to investigate why the initial infatuation often leads to an unsatisfactory marriage and then to a prolonged and painful separation. This book is an outgrowth of that dissertation more than it is of the relationship counseling I do.

My purpose in undertaking this work is to share what I have learned from my experiences as a Jungian analyst and relationship counselor about falling in and out of love. To be more specific, my purpose in writing this book is, first, to increase readers' awareness of themselves as persons with a tremendous potential to love and be loved, and second, to understand the meaning of their experiences with love. I also show the significance of one's ego and the proper place of the ego in one's psychic economy. The ego, of course, is not the only factor in the psyche, but it has an extremely important function; it is a conduit through which the rest of the personality may express itself. When we understand the relation of the ego to other psychic integrants, we are able to release those parts of ourselves that we might have kept bottled up.

Furthermore, I want to provide a kind of framework for imagining a fuller experience of one's life—which may not produce a better life as a result, but certainly a more interesting, if sometimes more painful one. But if the fuller life has more pain, it also has considerably more joy. In fact, the fuller life may have more of everything except boredom.

For readers who have had disappointing love affairs or marriages, I hope that this book will provide some understanding of why he or she fell in love with that particular person and what it was that doomed the relationship. One can read this book as a first step to change, that is, towards realizing that one must undertake a course of action that will bring about behavioral changes. This is not a do-it-yourself or a self-help book, but rather a *self-understanding* book. Reading it will, I hope, provide considerable enlightenment and perhaps some enjoyment, even though it contains no blueprints for carpentering a new personality, no prescription for selecting the "right" person with whom to fall in love, and no judgment about "what you have done wrong."

It is, I believe, the nonjudgmental nature of my observations of the phenomenon of infatuation or falling in love that differentiates this book from others. I know that there is no prescription for success in relationships and that there are no magic therapeutic techniques or sure-fire cures for dependency. I am no medicine man hawking fake panaceas. Nor am I going to tell anyone that particular ways of relating are dysfunctional, neurotic, or inappropriate.

I am bringing to this book the same objectivity that I bring to a client in analysis. This means that I have no preconceived notion of the meaning of the behaviors, attitudes, and experiences in relationships. Instead, I must ask, as I would clients in group therapy or analysis,

What is their aim?

What is their purpose?

What is their goal?

What wants expression in their behavioral and psychological activities before, during, and after two people fall in love?

When one knows the answers to these questions, one stands a relatively good chance of living a fuller and more rewarding life. In short, this book is about the *meaning* of falling in love; it is about the *need* to fall in love in order to become who and what we have the potential to be. It is about what in us falls in love and finds expression through our lover.

I have one bias that will permeate this book and which must, in all fairness to the reader, be expressed. I am on the side of the totality of the psyche. What I mean is that there is in us a lot of our Self of which we are purposefully and/or accidentally unconscious, and the totality of the psyche includes even those parts. To be on the side of the Self is to be on the side of the parts of us that we, personally and culturally, cannot or do not want to see. An extreme example would be our murderous impulses: it is essential that we know we have them but *not* that we should act on them. In fact, it is not knowing that one has such impulses that often leads to tragedies; if one knows the impulses are there, one can learn to contain them.

Another extreme is illustrated by one of my clients, Kay, who has been in a terrible and painful relationship for a decade now. She knows she needs to get out of it but she cannot. She is, in a sense, an addict. Although we can put a name to her problem, the label does her absolutely no good in terms of finding a way out of her dilemma. Even worse, the label gives her no understanding of herself and of what in her is being worked out through the relationship. Without that understanding, she would be likely, if she were to break loose from this lover, either to find another equally unsatisfying and destructive relationship, or, what would be just as bad, to shy away from other men out of fear of her addiction, like an alcoholic who dares not take that first drink.

The totality of the psyche needs relationships in order to fully express itself. Were Kay to abstain from relationships, she would have to repress or suppress an important part of her Self. Because I am on the side of the totality of the psyche, I do not want this part of her Self to be stifled for the rest of her life. At the same time, I want to encourage the development of those parts of her personality that are relatively independent and objective. I cannot, however, ask her to suppress or repress one or the other part of her personality. So we find ourselves in a quandary: Kay's "addiction" conflicts with her independence.

My bias might also be seen as extending to favor pain. But that would be a misunderstanding. I am not a sadist who wants to see people suffer, nor do I encourage people in general or clients in particular to seek out pain when none is present. What I am in favor of is suffering the pain that is natural to us as a result of who and what we are.

Another aspect of my bias is my strong belief in the value of those reflective and observant capabilities that we possess in such great measure and use so seldom. We receive little cultural support for observing ourselves; indeed, during adolescence, when Self-study is an important aspect of psychological development, teenagers are often accused of being narcissistic. We are born with the capacity to observe ourselves with both our outward and inward "eyes." We have been given imagination and intuition with which to receive and make use of information from our outer and inner worlds. I am also in favor of our capacity to collect information through reflection and observation.

Thus, in exploring this phenomenon of falling in love, my observations of and reflections on what occurs within and between humans in a romantic relationship are, as far as possible, devoid of cultural judgments. My years of working with couples in and out of relationships have made me recognize that what is normal in relationships is not necessarily what is socially acceptable.

What is normal in the human psyche is to project our fears, hopes, ideals, and dislikes onto other people (e.g., a child who has been brought up not to fear the dark requests a night light because his teddy bear is afraid of the dark). Projection is a psychic mechanism; it is the process by which we see in others, including inanimate objects and non-human beings, traits and qualities of which we are unconscious in our own personalities. One aspect of projection is blame—that is, ascribing to others responsibility for pain that more rightly belongs within ourselves. Projection is a very important psychological construct, and thus is discussed in some detail in Chapter III.

It is also normal for people who fall in love to experience joy in the relationship, to feel sadness, hurt, or disappointment, to become angry, to inhibit feelings, and to indulge in romantic or sexual fantasies about people outside the relationship. Socially acceptable behaviors in our culture, however, may not include feelings of hurt, sadness, and disappointment in a relationship, nor may they include being sexually aroused by a person outside the established relationship.

In sum, what is socially acceptable, in general, is a pattern of relating that distances us from the normal within us. What is socially acceptable in a relationship is public behavior. For example, in many states certain forms of sexual gratification between consenting adults, even in the privacy of their own homes, are illegal. Rage is not classed as illicit, yet the cultural proscription against it evokes guilt in people when they experience rage.

Generally, when people see rage in a relationship they do not interpret it as a normal mode of expressing intimacy. Because rage is not socially acceptable, to many people it must seem to be an unacceptable behavior. Ergo, if there is rage in the relationship then the relationship has something wrong with it and they try to fix it (an alternative to "fixing" the relationship might involve looking at what in the raging person is being protected by the anger). Just how difficult it can be to avoid culturally-conditioned ideals and judgments is apparent in the following example drawn from my analytic practice.

Sheila had been involved with a married man for several years. He had promised to marry her as soon as it was expedient for him to leave his wife, but Sheila was becoming impatient. Yet, as is often the case, he finally decided that he did not want to destroy his marriage, and instead broke off the affair with Sheila. She was terribly hurt and angry and almost overwhelmed by a sense of betrayal. Her only thought— indeed it became an obsession—was how to avenge herself, how to make him suffer as he had made her suffer. With me, her analyst, she could talk of little else: "Should I seek revenge? How? Should I tell his wife about the affair and how he betrayed her? Or should I seduce him one more time and then, when he takes the bait, reject him the way he rejected me?"

If I were to help her, I knew I needed to maintain my objectivity. But, in this case, what did objectivity mean? For example, I might have said, "You made your bed, now lie in it!" But this response would have been cultural (in our society marriages are sacrosanct and the "other woman" is a predator), not objective. My reaction would thus have reflected the cultural prejudice against extramarital affairs. On the other hand, I could not give her permission to seek revenge; that would not have been objective advice either, because in a sense I would have been sharing her feelings of betrayal and her fantasies of "getting even."

My position as an analyst dictated that I look at her questions from a psychological perspective: why was the thought of revenge so import- ant to her? In other words, if I were to be objective I would have to consider her thoughts of revenge as an important psychological content that must be understood before she can decide whether it is *permissible* for her to seek revenge. Therefore, I set about turning her thoughts to exploring her fantasies of revenge in order to understand *who* in her wanted to inflict hurt on her former lover. It could not be all of her psyche that wanted revenge, or she would most certainly have acted on the desire and not have sought permission or advice from me. The need for my approval indicated that she was beset by an inner moral and psychological dilemma that had to be raised to consciousness before she could make her own decision. Exploring her fantasies of revenge thus meant going deeper into her psyche and into her psychological processes.

Sheila's dilemma not only illustrates the value of an objective approach to psychological phenomena, but also provides an introduction to a part of ourselves that we either do not recognize or pay little attention to: the children in us. Even as mature adults we never leave behind the parts of ourselves that have come into being at different stages of development. For example, I remember a party at which an academician who was gaining national recognition said that every once in a while the seventeen-year-old adolescent within him looked at his nascent fame and marveled that it was happening. An artist in the group nodded in assent; he too experienced the same sense of wonderment from the adolescent within him. We are, however, far less aware of the young children in us, perhaps because they are buried so deep in our psyches. They tend to have left their permanent psychological imprint as the result of painful events that we have long forgotten but which are activated when a comparable situation arises.

In Sheila's case, the exploration of her desire for revenge revealed a small girl who had felt deprived of affection and attention. This child not only had been abandoned by Sheila's lover when he broke off the affair, but also had been abandoned by Sheila herself when she paid too little attention to this little girl's needs (in Chapter III we will look at the development of personality in order to understand the origins of the child in each of us). For now, it is only necessary to see how the little girl in Sheila had been abandoned in order to gain additional understanding of the useful function performed by objective observation.

There had been a number of occasions during the affair when Sheila had become painfully aware of the possibility that her lover might break off the relationship. Each time, the small girl within her would become frightened and insecure again, as we might expect. Instead of bringing this little girl to consciousness and attending to her by recognizing the destructive possibilities of the relationship, Sheila would focus on the behaviors that would bring her lover more pleasure, and perhaps bind him closer to her. In short, she concentrated on the lover instead of on the frightened little girl. Thus this inner child was abandoned at each step of the relationship, not only by the lover but by Sheila's conscious personality as well.

If Sheila's relationship and psychological problems seem complicated, rest assured that they are. I related them here to illustrate how very important the objective observation of psychological phenomena, even when difficult to achieve, is to being on the side of the totality of the personality. In Sheila's case, had I focused on her desire for revenge and how to achieve it, undoubtedly I would have short-circuited the possibilities for the other parts of her psyche; they would have been repressed if she had acted out her impulse for revenge.

The preceding discussion of objectivity also underlines why early in this introduction I noted that I would be as nonjudgmental and nonprescriptive in this book as I am in dealing with my clients. To judge someone's behavior implies a standard—perhaps legal, moral, or subjective—against which the behavior is judged. To prescribe implies laying down rules to change the behavior on the basis of some legal or moral criterion, or the initiation of therapy to "cure" the behavior based on medical or some objective theory. Neither judging nor prescribing is ever truly objective.

Throughout, we will thus pay particular attention to the meaning of involvement with a lover, what such involvements express in us, and the part we play in determining the nature of the involvement. In the process we will look at sexuality, insecurity, jealousy, playfulness, and other aspects of infatuation from an objective perspective to understand the genesis of such behaviors in the psyche and their purpose. We will also look at some constructs that are important to analytical psychology because they provide unique tools for understanding personalities and relationships.

About This Book

In Chapter II we look at the physical, emotional, psychological, and spiritual manifestations of the phenomenon of infatuation. They appear in spite of ourselves when we fall in love. Indeed, they seem to take over our lives as they change our behavior and perceptions of ourself, the person with whom we fall in love, and the world around us. These manifestations are the stuff of which poems and songs are made.

We also look at sexuality and its relation to love, and then at the emotions aroused by infatuation. These emotions may be painful as well as pleasant, but, because they are part of falling in love, we must be aware of them. To fall in love means to engage all mental, physiological, unconscious, and spiritual aspects of oneself.

Unfortunately, falling in love is often interpreted solely as a glandular or libidinal experience. This interpretation may be as much an effort to belittle the deep significance of love and relationships in our lives as it is to ignore spirituality or inspiration. Perhaps we accept such strictures because in our culture we consider discussions of nonmaterial phenomena outside of religion as embarrassing; indeed, we are probably conditioned against the examination of such topics from an early age because they are not "scientific." But love is not scientific. Unquestionably, many of us have had experiences that can only be described as spiritual or inspirational. Sometimes we change our way of thinking and our way of living as a result, but for fear of ridicule we neither speak of nor acknowledge the experiences openly.

Spirit, as it is discussed in relation to infatuation, has two separate manifestations, one ephemeral, the other concrete; the first may make itself known during infatuation and the second may determine the course of the resulting relationship.

My intent in Chapter II is to remove some of the embarrassment and shame from talking about what happens to us when we fall in love. We are so vulnerable at this point—our every nerve ending seems to be exposed—that we tend to be very cautious about describing the experience in full to others for fear that we will be considered too dependent, sex-crazed, prudish, blind to the other's faults, or violating some other social, but not natural, standard. Some people even try to deny the evidence of their senses for fear of disapproval by their peers. Whatever the cultural norm, when we fall in love we all feel insecure, anxious, obsessive, childlike, adolescent, and out of control, as well as other feelings we may not even be able to name. Knowing that these feelings are normal may relieve us of the anxiety stemming from the worry that we may be aberrant because of the way we feel and behave.

Why does infatuation affect us in such an unusual manner? The psychic source of our unusual feelings and behaviors is discussed in Chapter IV. However, in order to understand the complexity of that source it is necessary first to explore some of the structures and components of the personality. A brief exploration, therefore, is carried out in Chapter III. The theoretical orientation of my presentation is based on the work of Dr. Carl G. Jung, the Swiss analyst. Jung lived long enough to see many of his concepts not only adopted by psychoanalysts (Freudians) but, ironically, to see these claimed as extensions of Freud's psychological theories.

Thus after I describe the many aspects of the personality in Chapter III, including the processes of the unconscious, I show how they influence one's early development. That influence and the weight of culture work together to fill out one's adult personality. From the interaction of the two, we can understand why and how we fall in love with a particular person at a particular time.

Although infatuation is "normal," we have to enter the complicated and cloudy world of unconscious processes to understand why we fall in love and why we seem to select a particular kind of person with whom to fall in love. A complete discussion would take many more pages—volumes, in fact—than this book provides. So, in Chapter III, I concentrate on only those principles essential to an understanding of the deep psychological processes lying at the root of infatuation.

One reason I am attached to this chapter is that it is my means of attacking the myriad of present-day "how-to" or "self-help" psychology books that describe in an accusatory manner such phenomena as "sexual addiction," "men who hate women," "women who are dependent on men," "co-dependency," and the like, and then brusquely tell the reader (prescribe), "Stop it!" Part of my antipathy to such materials arises from their potential for damage to the psychologically less informed reader. Here is an example from my clinical practice.

Ann, a middle-aged mother of three, and married for a number of years, came into my consulting room with an anxious expression. She had been reading one of the popular "how-to" books on women in relationships. One of the problems in her marriage was that once or twice a month her husband came home late for dinner. The author of her "how-to" book recommended, "Don't let yourself get angry; just go ahead and eat. Don't nag at him or show anger because he is late." Now that is good advice if you can follow it. But what of the person, like my client, who couldn't repress her anger?

The night before, her husband had been late and Ann did not wait for him but sat down to eat dinner with the children at the usual time. When he arrived home she was angry that he had not called, but she tried not to show it and she did not nag. At her regular appointment she was still angry and she also felt guilty about its persistence. We explored the source of her anger: whenever her husband was late (he had a long drive home), Ann couldn't help worrying about whether something had happened to him. What was the basis of her fear for his safety? Her love for him. Why was she angry? He refused to call to reassure her.

Thus, in her case, the author's prescription was harmful rather than helpful. If Ann were to act out the author's advice to stop feeling what would make her a nag, she would have to repress her anger out of consciousness, withdraw from her husband until she had done so, and lose contact with her fear as well as her love for him—because both would have been replaced by an unconscious or conscious resentment. The nature of resentment is such that the relationship between Ann and her husband would have been damaged more by the feelings of resentment than by her anger and nagging, which were one of the ways she showed her love for him. This is a part of Ann's nature, and we cannot know what it means for to express her love and fear this way unless we take an objective look at its goal.

There is a more complex answer to why we cannot accept an external ideal without critically examining its effect on us, and that answer is explored throughout this book. I stated earlier that I am on the side of the totality of the psyche, and am consequently opposed to repression. A second purpose of Chapter III is thus to analyze the complexity of psychic activity and to warn against the dangers of uncritically accepting generalized advice on psychic matters.

In Chapter IV, the personality theory discussed in Chapter III is connected to the behaviors described in Chapter II. In other words, Chapter II describes *what* happens when we fall in love; Chapter IV tells us *why* it happens. So Chapter IV is a theoretical analysis of the intrapsychic process of infatuation. In a way, the chapter can be likened to a map that details the topography of the unconscious world during infatuation, and reveals the functions of its processes.

We move, in a sense, into the midst of that unconscious world in Chapter V. The dreams and their interpretations (taken from the case study of a woman I will call "Harriet") that make up the contents of the chapter illuminate what goes on in the unconscious during a critical period in Harriet's infatuation with her lover ("Hans"). The unconscious tends to "speak" through images rather than voices, and the images have a universal nature that must be interpreted in light of the dreamer's experiences. Some of the figures that appear in Harriet's dreams are clearly aspects of her ego or other parts of her personality. Some figures represent bits of herself which she has known and lost touch with, people she has known and hated, or those who abandoned her during formative years, as well as attitudes that have been incorporated into her personality. We will see how infatuation propels her into a nether world where past and present merge with the future, where she is accosted by personality traits she would prefer not to acknowledge, and where the morality of her cultural milieu conflicts with her personal integrity. In Harriet's unconscious world, we see suggestions of the unconscious processes that take her down from the euphoria of infatuation into, first, the boredom of an everyday relationship and then, inexorably, into a blacker, more painful conflict-filled separation.

The dreams and interpretations presented in Chapter V are directed to readers who have little experience with dream interpretation in general or with Jungian dream interpretation in particular. Those with the necessary background and experience are referred to the Endnotes to Chapter V, where the interpretations are more complete. I have made use of the *Rosarium philosophorum*,[1] an alchemical text taken from Jung's seminal work, *The Psychology of the Transference*, to illustrate the course of infatuation.

The purpose of separating the technical interpretation in the Endnotes from the interpretations in Chapter V is to make the essential content of the book accessible to all readers, but at the same time to make the results of my researches available to my colleagues in analytical psychology. Although the contents of the Endnotes may be somewhat theoretical in nature, I have tried to couch my discussions in nontechnical language as much as possible so as not to shut out those lay readers who are interested in exploring the expanded dream interpretations. Chapter VI concentrates on the dynamics of marriage and separation; Chapter VII, on the process of reunion.

Introduction to Alchemy

Jung, like the scientists and scholars of his day, received a classical education; hence he, like them, was able to read and understand early and medieval Latin without difficulty. One of his lifelong interests was hunting down, in libraries and from collectors of antiquaries, ancient manuscripts or copies of them. Because of his psychiatric training, he was especially interested in works relating to illness and medications. This interest led him to old tomes on alchemy, the study of the chemistry of metals that was started by the Egyptians, advanced by Greek and Arabian scholars, and then carried through Spain to Western Europe. Alchemists engaged in such processes as trying to transmute base metals (e.g., lead) to "noble" ones (e.g., gold or silver), and later to develop a practical pharmacopedia. In histories of science, alchemy is usually treated as the predecessor of modern-day chemistry.

Throughout its history, alchemy was based on philosophical principles. Among the Greeks, for example, it was linked to theories of matter. In alchemical writings, Jung found an esoteric philosophy which he believed contained fundamental images of our psychic life.

My interest in the connection between relationships and alchemy was aroused when I saw a series of pictures in one alchemical tract, the *Splendor Solis*.[2] Like many other alchemical tracts in which the alchemist describes his formula for the transmutation of minerals and metals into gold, the *Splendor Solis* utilizes pictures to enhance the meaning of alchemical processes. Pictures were apparently used to describe, in image form, concepts which the intellect and words seemed unable to articulate. In my first semester of training at the C. G. Jung Institute in Zurich, I took a class on the interpretation of dreams. After we had covered the basics, the instructor, a wizened old man trained by Jung himself, asked for volunteers to interpret several dream series. Being naive, I raised my hand; I had no idea that I was expected to write a paper interpreting the series assigned to me and then to read the paper before the whole class for criticisms and comments.

For the next few weeks I studied the dreams and took notes. Finally, I uncovered a thread that seemed to tie the dreams together. I wrote my interpretation and then let it "sit" for several days. During that period, however, I became increasingly dissatisfied with my explication because of what seemed to be a paradox between the dreamer's conscious life and her dreams. She was thirty-five years old, well-educated, and employed in a responsible position. Her life was orderly and she was apparently fulfilling her career role admirably, yet her dreams were filled with horrid images, as if she were moving inexorably toward a personality dissolution of dangerous proportions. My interpretation, it seemed to me, did not adequately explain the paradox.

One afternoon, I sat on the couch in my apartment stewing over the problem. To relieve my tension, I went to a bookshelf and pulled out a book, *The Splendor Solis*, which I had bought several years earlier but had never examined. All good Jungians have at least one book on alchemy, if only to show that they too can be esoteric, and this book was mine. As I leafed through the slim volume, I noticed a picture that reminded me of one of the images in the dream series. The similarity piqued my curiosity, so I looked further. Several other pictures also showed a similarity. So I began to read the text. Gradually, I began to see that the images—which appeared to suggest a personality dissolution in the dreamer—were not indications of pathology, but rather the traces of the unconscious at work purposefully restructuring her conscious personality. This insight seemed monumental to me. "So this," I thought, "is what Jung was onto when he studied alchemy!" Thus I learned that alchemy is about the reconstruction of the personality, about the process of individuation.

In his autobiography, *Memories, Dreams, Reflections,*[3] Jung attributes to his study of alchemy the clarification of "the central concept" of his psychology:

> In "The Relationship between the Ego and the Unconscious" I had discussed only my preoccupation with the unconscious, and something of the nature of that preoccupation, but had not yet said anything much about the unconscious itself. As I worked with my fantasies, I became aware that the unconscious undergoes or produces change. Only after I had familiarized myself with alchemy did I realize that the unconscious is a *process*, and that the psyche is transformed or developed by the relationship of the ego to the contents of the unconscious. In individual cases that transformation can be read from dreams and fantasies. In

collective life it has left its deposit principally in the various religious systems and their changing symbols. Through the study of these collective transformation processes and through understanding of alchemical symbolism I arrived at the central concept of my psychology: *the process of individuation.*[4] (p. 209)

The idea of individuation, according to Henri Ellenberger, the historian of the development of modern psychiatry, was first enunciated by Pindar, the Latin odist, in the precept, "Become what thou art."[5] Ellenberger also provides a concise explication of how Jung related alchemy to psychology. What Jung found in the alchemical writings was:

> . . . a projection of the process of individuation in the series of operations performed by alchemists. Just as Jung's patients materialized their dreams and fantasies in the form of drawings and paintings, the alchemists materialized their own processes of individuation in the form of pseudo-chemical operations. It is also the reason, Jung adds, why accounts of visions are often to be found in the writings of alchemists.[6]

My fascination with the connection between relationships and alchemy intensified with I saw pictures from the *Rosarium philosophorum*. One of the first pictures in the tract shows a crowned king and queen holding hands. It reminded me of my own wedding; during the ceremony, crowns were placed on our heads and my left and my wife's right arm were wrapped, joining us.

In alchemical literature, the king and queen are important symbols of the masculine and feminine properties of metals. The interplay and interaction between "masculine" and "feminine" metals and minerals played the essential part in the "creation" of gold. This book is intended to demonstrate the linkage between outer experience of infatuation with a person of the opposite sex and the intrapsychic experience of encountering the other parts of our personality of which we are unconscious. And as with alchemy, the goal is the creation of something (ourselves and our relationships) which is precious, soft and yet immutable (masculine properties were seen as active, spiritual, penetrating; feminine properties, as receptive, "soul-full"). Jung likened metal to personality and hypothesized that, as a consequence of the psychological mechanism of projection, what the alchemists were seeing in the metals and the processes of transmuting them were fundamental psychological processes and images that had to do with transforming the personality from a state of unconsciousness (base metal) to consciousness (gold).

If we can accept the idea that the gold the alchemist desires is, in fact, individuation, or the creation and transformation of the personality, then the processes used by the alchemists would be unconscious projections of the images and processes of individuation. In other words, the alchemists saw in the transformation of metals the images and processes by which individuals transform themselves. However, the images and processes must be viewed as symbols that need to be interpreted— better yet, translated—just as dream images must be if we are to understand their meanings.

The image of the king and queen, then, represents parts of ourselves that are active and receptive, spiritual and soulful. As our discussion progresses, we will see that in relationships activity/receptivity and spirituality/soulfulness, in all their respective facets, play a remarkable role in the attraction, formation, equilibrium, separation, and reunion of two people in love.

I want to make clear that alchemical images and processes are a metaphor for the objective imagining of the experiences of relationships. If alchemy is anything other than the fantastic mutterings of greedy and disturbed eccentrics, then it is the study of psychology, relationships, and individuation projected into the metals upon which the alchemists performed their obscure formulae. The *Rosarium* is thus more than a description of chemical processes. It is a symbolic representation of the inner processes of individuation, the external indications of which appear in infatuation, marriage and separation. We will see that infatuation with a member of the opposite sex corresponds with the alchemical stage of the initial *coniunctio* (conjunction), which is the external indication that something unconscious is being stirred to activity, the goal of which is to become conscious.

Now, of course, we must address the last and most important question about the study of alchemical imagery, namely the use to which this knowledge is put in the consulting room. Jung, in contrast to Freud, focused upon the study of the normal, that is, on what is normal in the human psyche. I too am concerned with human normality, but more narrowly, with what is normal in human relationships. We will see in this book, just as we do in Jung's works, that what is normal in the human psyche is not always what is socially acceptable.

Some degree of jealousy is normal in relationships, although jealousy is neither pleasant to experience nor to observe. If we did not have evidence that jealousy is normal, we might all surrender to the illusion, a common one in our culture, that there is something "wrong" in feeling jealous. More to the point is the assertion that love is blind. When we are no longer in love we know that we were blind when we were in love. However, when we are in love we are sure that we are not blind.

Three explanations for this phenomenon come to mind: (a) that we are in fact not blind when we are in love but that we see the world differently; (b) that we are blind when we are in love but will not admit it because we have had impressed upon us the idea that there is something wrong with being blindly in love; and (c) that we do not know that we are blind when we are in love.

Let me assert right now that all three explanations are correct. The dreams I present in Chapter V will assist us in seeing how three apparently contradictory explanations can be equally valid at the same time.

Alchemy and the Psychology of Archetypes

Jung used alchemy in his researches to identify patterns of perception and images that seemed to be common to all humanity. He found similarities between these images and patterns and the information coming out of the work of both anthropologists and mythologists, two fields of study that were expanding rapidly at that time. This information, when combined with his own studies, led him to conclude that there are, in the psyche, unconscious principles that order everyday experience and provide the framework for the perception of everyday experiences. He called these ordering principles archetypes, from the Greek *archon* (ruling principles) and *typos* (pattern or standard). Jung saw the archetypes as magnetic poles that draw experiences together and make them coherent parts of our life. The account of this discovery is found in Jung's writings and in his 1959 interview on the BBC program "Face to Face."

One day, at the Burghölzli Psychiatric Hospital in Zurich where Jung worked for some years, a long-time patient stopped him in the corridor and begged him to come look out the window. Jung obliged. Pointing excitedly at the sun, the patient said the sun had a phallus swinging from side to side and this swinging caused the wind. Jung thought the image was the raving of an uneducated paranoid-schizophrenic and let the matter drop. Several years later, however, he found a recently published translation of some old codex on Mithraic liturgy that attributed the occurrence of the wind to a swinging tube hanging down from the sun. Upon checking, Jung found that the patient could not have seen the book before he was hospitalized (it had not been translated at that time) and certainly had not had access to the book in the hospital. How was it, then, that he "saw" the same image a liturgical writer had described centuries earlier?

Delving deeper into the unconscious psyche through the dreams, fantasies, and associations of his patients, Jung saw the emergence of images and symbols that formed patterns of perception; they indicated to him that humans come equipped with a common *possibility* for perception. If one accepts the fact that certain behaviors are instinctual and that the source of the instincts may well be in our evolutionary development, then it is not unlikely that certain patterns of perception should have the same source. Thus Jung began to hypothesize the existence of an impersonal unconscious—he termed it the "collective unconscious"—made up of the archetypes that contain the possibility for perceptions (such as the source of the wind). The existence of the collective unconscious and archetypes goes a long way toward explaining similarities of perception across cultures and times, such as mythological characters and motifs, fairy tales, religious rituals, and descriptions of the people with whom we fall in love as well as those whom we hate and fear.

One of the archetypes identified by Jung as a result of his studies of alchemy was that of individuation, the drive which impels us toward consciously becoming all that we can be. Part of the process of individuation, Jung saw, is the work of bringing unconscious contents into consciousness, that is, personality traits that are unacceptable to us and so have been repressed, as well as traits that we have never seen in ourselves before. The dependent woman I mentioned earlier, whose dream of the Amazon helped her to identify a more independent part of herself with which she could make contact and so live out in the world, is a case in point.

Through the concept of individuation, Jung was describing an apparently natural psychic process whose goal is to expand our experience of ourselves. The theory of archetypes is amply supported by historical, anthropological, and mythical information, both in process and image. That is, Jung found similarities between images and processes among alchemical, mythological, anthropological, and historical materials, and the dream images of his patients.

Two of the archetypes other than individuation which Jung examined in detail were the *anima* ("soul") and *animus* ("spirit"). They are discussed in detail in Chapter III because they are the psyche's key actors in infatuation. Suffice to say that the anima and animus have two fundamental properties, one as a function and the other as content. In their functional aspect the anima and animus mediate between the unconscious and conscious; for example, when we are "animated," we are in touch with something unconscious in us, but capable of becoming conscious.

The content of the anima and animus is the total collection of all the images of the opposite (and the same, for some figures) sex that we have absorbed throughout our lives. Over the following chapters, we will observe the interplay of consciousness, unconsciousness, and anima and animus in relationships and in the process of individuation.

NOTES

1. *Rosarium philosophorum*. Frankfurt first edition, 1550 (woodcuts). Textual quotations, however, are taken from revisions printed in *Art. Aurif.*, II (Basel, 1593). Cited in: Jung, C. G., *The Practice of Psychotherapy*. New York: Princeton University Press, 1954, pp. 203 ff.

2. *Ibid.*, pp. 163 ff.

3. S. Trismosen, *The Splendor Solis*. London: Kegan Paul, Trench, Trubner & Co., Ltd., 1582. Reprinted by Yoga Publication Society, Des Plaines, Illinois (no date).

4. C. G. Jung, *Memories, Dreams, Reflections*. New York: Vintage Books, 1965, p. 209.

5. H. Ellenberger, *The Discovery of the Unconscious*. New York: Basic Books, 1970, p. 718.

6. *Ibid.*, pp. 719-20.

CHAPTER II

ANIMATION

Come live with me and be my love
And we will all the pleasures prove . . .
The Passionate Shepherd (1589)
Christopher Marlowe

Our passions are most like to floods and
streams . . .
The Silent Lover (1600)
Sir Walter Raleigh

Falling in love or becoming infatuated with a person is not an act of conscious will—it happens to us. Sometimes it happens suddenly (love at first sight), sometimes during a friendship, and sometimes during a long-standing intimate relationship that seems to have gone stale.

Proximity is not a necessary condition. Adolescents and lonely persons often become infatuated with people they have seen only in the movies or on television screens. And suitability is not essential. One of the oldest themes in literature is the consequences of inappropriate infatuations: Paris and Helen, King David and Bathsheba, Tristram and Isolde, and Scarlett and Ashley. Why we fall in love or with whom we fall in love is not and cannot be directed by the ego.

We must distinguish between *infatuation* (falling in love) and *love*, since the two are often confused. They are alike only in that both are unstructured phenomena (i.e., we know them only through experience)

23

and both involve an "other." The major difference between them is that infatuation is a finite period of passion and the awakening of dormant parts of one's personality, whereas love is a reality-oriented commitment and deep-rooted devotion. Given the subjective nature of infatuation and love, precise definitions are difficult. We might say at the outset, however, that in the former we love our projections on the other person, while in the latter we love the person on whom we have projected. This perhaps cryptic definition will become much clearer by the end of Chapter III.

From the psychological perspective, the nearest we can come to defining love is to say that it is a numinous experience—spiritual and mysterious—that surpasses comprehension and arouses elevated or spiritual emotions. When one loves another person, one is manifesting "a dominant or regular disposition or tendency; [a] prevailing character or quality . . . [Love is] an acquired behavior pattern regularly followed until it has become almost involuntary" (*The Random House College Dictionary*).

Infatuation is also involuntary and unpatterned, but it is differentiated from love by extravagant passion. All of one's sexuality and emotions are aroused in an infatuation. No matter how long one may have known a person, when one becomes infatuated with him or her the person suddenly is imbued with mystery. Thus, psychologically, infatuation is the initial state of attraction that provides the energy for exploring the mystery of the other.

Infatuation can be the beginning of a long-term attachment or of a temporary flare-up of passion that cools down almost as quickly as it began. It is blind and unreasoning, and thus often may be foolish and irrational. It can lead to love or it can end in disappointment. It is a period of thralldom. Infatuated lovers are ready to give up everything for each other, sometimes even their lives. Infatuation is Romeo stabbing himself when he believes that Juliet is dead and then her committing suicide when she sees his lifeless body. It is King Edward VIII giving up the throne of the British Empire to marry the American divorcée, Mrs. Wallis Simpson. Infatuation is the stuff of romance that precedes the fairy tale ending, "and they lived happily ever after."

Infatuation manifests itself in a variety of behaviors, some conventional and some bizarre, but all energized by forces over which the lovers have no conscious control. The behaviors run the gamut from ecstasy to agony and are triggered by feelings far deeper than any the lovers may ever have experienced before. Even the agony can be tolerated, however, because it makes one aware of one's heightened feelings and of the joy of being alive.

Indeed, during an infatuation we feel as if every fiber of our being has suddenly been vitalized. Our senses are sharpened: hearing is more acute; vision is clearer; and our skin is more sensitive to every touch. Our blood seems to be hotter and to run faster. Our bodies take on new powers. Our energy seems to be boundless. We may be shocked by desires to act aggressively or to be masochistic. Our world seems to be topsy-turvy, and, at the same time, filled with magic. Time seems to stand still or to accelerate depending on whether we are apart or together. The present seems to stretch ahead endlessly and the past lives again. Our feelings are overwhelming. We know there has never been love like ours—love is our discovery—and there never can be such love again. We need to prove the reality of the other by touching and being touched, and we need to reveal ourselves through our confidences. We fear losing each other, and the fear is as strong as if separation were about to occur. The world exists only to hold us and our love. It seems to pulse to our rhythm.

The source of infatuation is in certain integrants of the psyche or personality. They are universal unconscious contents that exist in all people but differ depending on the early influences in our lives, the environment in which we have grown up, our psychological and cognitive development, and our life experiences. Thus, although the structures and interrelations of our psychic integrants may be identical, the contents of the integrants are unique to each of us and thus give each of us a unique personality.

We experience these integrants only partially in the conscious state (in consciousness). The psyche, which is discussed in detail in Chapter III, consists of the integrants, functions, and components that act and interact variously at different levels of the unconscious and consciousness. The psyche itself is a unity, however, and we can say, a continuum of constant psychic activity.

The particular psychic functions we are concerned with in this chapter are feeling, instinct, and spirit. They have deep connections to our unconscious, so deep that many people live out their lives without being aware of their instincts and spirit and know their feeling function only at a superficial level. Some people are uncomfortable with the idea of integrants and functions, and thus try to equate them with the stuff of philosophy, poetry, or religion. Yet they are as much a part of us as our skin and bones; indeed, they manifest their existence in our dreams and in many of our behaviors, especially those related to infatuation and love.

FEELING

In the following discussion, the word "feeling" will refer to emotions, moods, affects, and temperament.[1] It is what we mean when we say, in response to certain circumstances resultant from inner and/or outer events, "I feel hurt" or "I feel sad." Four common feelings are: hurt, sadness, disappointment, and joy.

Feelings have a purpose. Like our intellect, senses, and intuition, feelings provide us with information about our current state. They are another means of perceiving our environment. We are often unaware that something is happening to us until we have a feeling and then, upon reflection, we see that the feeling was telling us something about ourselves in relation to the situation. In our culture, for the most part, feelings and emotions are regarded with suspicion; they are often equated with feminine weakness. Yet as we proceed through this book, we shall see that we are partially blinded to ourselves and our world when we try to disavow our feelings and emotions.

We have attained a certain consciousness about ourselves when we can predict our emotional reactions to particular events: sadness when we must say goodbye to a good friend; joy when we anticipate being with a lover; disappointment if, for example, the seats to a concert we want to attend are sold out. It is equally important, when we have an emotional reaction and do not know its source, to reflect on what has brought that reaction into being. By doing so we expand or add to the consciousness of ourselves and our world. One of the saddest things in life, for many people, is to recognize happiness only when it is past.

It is not unusual for people to listen to and accept the information given to them by pleasurable emotions and feelings (e.g., love, excitement, joy) but to disregard those painful feelings that may have even more to say. One of my clients, for example, was so excited by the prospect of earning a relatively large salary on a promotion he was offered that he paid no attention to his dislike and fear for the person who would be his new supervisor. As soon as he moved into his new role, however, he discovered he could do nothing to please the supervisor, and sadly, was soon fired.

Our feelings should be distinguished from other experiences that are popularly referred to as "feelings." For instance, when we say we have a "feeling" that something terrible will happen soon, we are actually talking about an intuition. And when we say we "feel as if we have been run over by a truck," we are, in fact, using a metaphor to describe our reaction to an experience. The metaphor itself is not a "feeling."

I limit the use of "feeling" in this book to a very specific emotional experience that expresses relatedness to a person or situation in one's inner or outer world. In other words, the feelings discussed in this section are those that describe a sense of relatedness to and with one's inner and outer experiences of people and circumstances. For example, a woman may feel "hurt" by the thoughtless comment of her lover because his opinions are important to her; and we usually feel "sad" when a friend suffers a misfortune because we relate to what the loss or accident must mean to the friend as well as to the feelings the friend must be going through. In the same way, in the ongoing relationship with our Self (i.e., our total personality), we may feel "sad" or "disappointed" when we do or say something that is contrary to our personal values. The important aspect of feeling, as the term is used here, is that it is usually related to the Self or other person(s). Anger is not technically a feeling in our definition, but an emotional and physiological response best categorized as an instinctive reaction to perceived threat. When one becomes angry one often "sees red": one's adrenal glands are activated, and one becomes ready to fight.

I have avoided so far talking about guilt and shame, since these are strong emotions qualitatively different from the feelings I have been talking about. Like anger, guilt and shame stem from conflict, not relatedness. That is, they are engendered by the conflict between our nature and/or behavior and the unquestioned expectations we hold for our actions. Thus from my viewpoint guilt and shame are meant to restrict what is in our nature. We also can characterize guilt and shame as emotions that express the expectations of our families, schools, religious beliefs, and communities under certain circumstances. In a sense, these emotions have the effect of isolating us. They separate us from relating, on the one hand, to our Self and our nature; on the other hand, they do not permit us to relate to those individuals and institutions that have evoked the inhibiting force from which our shame and guilt stem. These two strong emotions then, do not bring us into relation with ourselves or others, but instead, act as emotional inhibitors.

True feelings—sadness, disappointment, hurt, and joy—have full reign during an infatuation. Love activates and sensitizes people to express their feelings to a greater extent and depth and richness than they knew were possible. And lovers have a compelling need to spend hours reminiscing about their past lives because pleasant and unpleasant memories are reactivated and relived.

Several clients have told me that they have taken new lovers to their home towns or neighborhoods to show them where they had grown up and gone to school, and once there they spilled out recollections of those early years, as if a hidden store suddenly had been discovered.

The recounting of memories serves the purpose of incorporating the new lover into one's history.

New-found love also activates fresh responses to old sights and events. The whole world seems to have been refurbished for the lovers and to have acquired delights the lovers never noticed before. The most commonplace objects sparkle with a hitherto unnoticed beauty that seems to mirror the beauty of their relationship. Ordinary activities and events are imbued with mysterious delights.

The early intimacy when love first blooms is of great importance. Arising in the emotions and affects, it signifies that something unusual and special is happening. It is invariably true that love brings with it a lowering of one's usual level of secrecy. Lovers have almost a childlike trust in each other. The result is long hours of intimate discussions about feelings, personal tragedies and triumphs, faux pas, confessions, and ruminations. It is why intelligence agencies place such a high value on the bedroom as a source of information.

Lovers have a great need to reveal themselves to each other, to trust and be trusted. Personal histories, desires, tastes, hobbies, goals, and friends and families all take on greater meaning when lovers talk about them and begin the process that brings each into the life of the other. This mutual identification is the way lovers assimilate and are assimilated by each other. Intimacy brings ardent feelings of peace, unity, and comradeship with this one person in the world who understands and cares.

The entire feeling life of lovers is renewed, revitalized. They feel an openness to ideas and places and people far beyond the boundaries within which they had previously carried on their lives. The walls of habit are penetrated and tumble down. The lovers talk about new ideas and aspirations. They do things and enjoy activities they had never considered before. So lovers of classical music find themselves responding to rock music when they are in love, and shy individuals approach new people and situations with confidence.

The lovers also find they cannot bear to part. When they are separated for a day, a week, or an hour, they are lonely and feel incomplete. Yet the loneliness is not relieved by other people. Lovers abandon friends and interests that hitherto had been important because they want to be alone with each other. The desire for seclusion is as much an expression of loss of interest in the outer world as of the feeling that they must guard their budding relationship from real or imagined outside threats.

Loss of interest in the world is actually a concentration of energy in the building and solidifying of the relationship. In a sense, lovers become addicted to the sight and sound of each other. Each fears losing the other and views the world and its people as threats to the fragile relationship.

One of my analysands, Don, displayed a classic example of this fear. He had fallen quickly and deeply in love with June and could not bear the thought of being parted from her. She had arranged, before they met, to visit a cousin in another city. Don became obsessed with the fear that June might meet a more attractive and persuasive man there and be swept off her feet. He used all the arguments he could muster to convince her that he should accompany her on the trip. When he told me of the incident later, he felt certain that his primary reason for wanting to go with her was to avoid a painful separation, one that he knew he could not endure. After we examined this rationale, however, he realized that the pain he had anticipated was the fear of losing June to someone else.

Such feelings of insecurity and fear of loss are not unusual during infatuations, and they have very little to do with the psychological condition of the people concerned. Certainly, a pathological condition will exaggerate the intensity of feelings, but it will not create them. These feelings are the emotional expression of an unconscious process present in everyone and activated when one falls in love.

Some people, when they are aware of the unmitigated bliss they feel during an infatuation, cannot help wondering if they have a right to such happiness. Margie, another analysand, started consulting me because she was depressed and unhappy with her life. Then, at the beginning of a session some months later, she told me she had fallen in love. Her depression seemed to lift almost miraculously. She felt alive and invigorated. But two weeks later, when she came to see me, she was frightened. What if these feelings did not last? What if her lover left her or was accidentally killed?

The threat of impending doom often overcomes lovers, especially when they seem to have reached heights of passion and fulfillment they had never known before. Many couples talk about their mutual insecurities and try to comfort each other.

It is easy for psychologists, amateur or professional, to sit back and sagely hold forth on the unresolved mother or father complex and dependency needs that drive people to fall in love with each other. But men and women never fall in love deliberately—were they able to do so there would be fewer lonely people in the world—and the psychological processes that stimulate the infatuation are very intricate.

Over the decades, newspapers and scandal sheets have regaled readers with reports of so-called misalliances: heiresses falling in love with chauffeurs; scions becoming infatuated with prostitutes; and psychologists and psychiatrists having affairs with patients despite their professional codes of conduct. And every once in a while a member of the clergy takes a married parishioner or young adult as a lover, to the horror of the congregation.

There is in such people no conscious intent to violate the mores of their callings or the expectations of their families. They become infatuated with particular persons because of something primal, something that is not adapted to the collective standard of behavior and that is not under the control of one's conscious defenses. Their behavior, in other words, has been dictated not by logic or "oughts," but by their instincts and spirit as well as by feelings they cannot control.

INSTINCTS

Instincts are inborn patterns of behavior. I use the term to designate those psychological processes that are part of everyone's psyche, namely, the need for relationships, sexuality, and aggression. The instincts do not include biological functions (e.g., hunger, vision, digestion, fatigue) because they have no psychological content in themselves or in relation to others. Nevertheless, purely biological functions may represent psychological contents or have symbolic meanings in, for example, dreams and fantasies.

Need for Relationships

In the early days of an infatuation, the instinctive contents are activated around sexuality and the relationship, and are focused directly on the lover. A wealth of sociological, anthropological, and psychological evidence confirms the universality of the need for relationships. In fact, many higher primates (e.g., chimpanzees and apes) display personal as well as social relationships. Here I shall present only brief notes from the voluminous data, starting with two compelling and obvious facts.

First, human beings create culture, and culture requires personal relationships for purposes of procreation, continuity of the group, and social relations (i.e., social organization) for purposes of mutual protection and defense. These facts are undisputed and illustrate the instinctive urge among humans to relate to one another.

The second and equally compelling instance arises out of a cultural paradox. On one hand, culture requires a certain conformity among its members in order to survive and prosper. On the other hand, as culture develops there evolves a certain collective attitude that bestows value and respect upon individuals who transcend the instinctive need for relationships and, instead, embark on a solitary journey through life. Classic examples are hermits who spend years on mountaintops or in deserts contemplating the nature of the cosmos, and monks and nuns who withdraw hermitically into their visionary experiences. Because they are exceptions to accepted social behavior, we can infer that they are valued precisely because they stand in opposition to our instinctive nature.

When we agree that the need for relationships is instinctive, we must also agree with the corollary: that actions threatening the instinctive behavior will stimulate a reaction and lead to the feeling and affective states noted earlier. Thus if our nature is to need relationships, then it is also our nature to play an active role in seeking them and trying to preserve them when they are threatened.

The dominant culture, however, dictates how we should act out our instinctual needs. In some societies the instincts are taken for granted. It is assumed that individuals will want to express their sexuality, and societies thus regularize how this basic instinct will be expressed. Until recently in the United States, the dominant culture seemed to try to deny the existence of instincts. Indeed, behaviorism, the school of thought that dominated American psychology for many decades, expounded the belief that all behaviors are learned and that all habits stem from conditioned physiological reactions. Because of cultural dictates, people were implicitly taught to play down their instinctive needs.

Until recently, it was taboo for a woman to overtly pursue a relationship with a man. It is commonplace, according to many of the letters received by Ann Landers or Dear Abby, for a husband to fail to tell his spouse over the years that he loves and cares for her, as if there were something shameful in expressing his need for her. Such behaviors place a high value on independence (i.e., not admitting that the husband needs his wife at the feeling level) and on hiding one's instinctive need for relationship, except under certain conditions.

Sexuality

Sexuality differs from love, although both are instinctual. The first usually refers to the totality of a person's sexual attitudes, desires, tendencies, and behaviors, whereas the second is the feeling of connection one has to another person in a relationship that may or may not be expressed sexually. The expression of sexuality "is one manifestation of the need for love and union," as Erich Fromm put it.[2]

Whether actual or fantasied, sexuality is activated in a fundamental opposition. To a man the lover is seen as a virgin, yet at the same time there lurks in the back of his mind the deep-seated fear that she is, in fact, a whore. A woman may see her lover as a protective and resourceful man, yet images of him as a bacchanalian satyr come frequently to her mind. He feels a strong sexual attraction for her; she seems to be pure, untouched by other men, a virgin who has held herself in readiness only for him. The woman feels that he has never loved anyone as he loves her. These feelings are present even when both have had previous sexual experiences and know about them. The lovers' respective histories are obviously not an overly important factor.

At the same time, certain fears also are activated. She is mine now, but will she be mine tomorrow? next week? next month? The reason is that in any strong attraction vague suspicions coalesce into the attraction's opposite, the threat of loss. To him, it means literally the loss to another man. Thus, the virgin becomes a prostitute, not by her behavior but in his fantasies. Much the same process occurs in her, although she has many more fantasies to deal with because our culture has constructed a much more elaborate mythology about men and their sexuality: men are easily aroused, they cannot control their sexual urges and they are at the mercy of their instincts. Thus men tend to be unfaithful. They court women only for sexual gratification and then discard them. Men are naturally polygamous.

The effects of unfaithfulness, whether actual or fantasied, are encountered in the consulting rooms of analysts and marriage counselors every day. It is also the implicit stimulus for confidences between friends. He tells his chum how blissfully happy he is with his new love, but is it to share his joy or to suppress his fear that she may abandon him for a rival yet unknown? She tells a confidante how happy and secure her lover makes her feel, but she doesn't dare reveal her terror that he may be making a fool of her by carrying on with someone else behind her back. Such fears are usually expressed only in consulting rooms or in dreams.

Aggression and Sexuality

It is easy enough to identify how the instinctive needs for relationship and sexuality are satisfied in the early stages of a love affair—but not aggression. Although it is as much a part of infatuation as sexuality, aggression generally does not manifest itself so soon. Our society does not tolerate aggression well, and its lack of appearance is even a yardstick by which we are meant to judge the quality of a relationship. Just as aggression is given little direct expression in our daily lives (except by individuals we consider criminals), so too is it given little expression in the first stages of a relationship.

By consensus, aggression is defined as crude, violent, uncivilized, and uncontrolled behavior. Anger, which is one form of aggression, is hidden away in the secret places of one's psyche where it cannot be seen by others. To be angry is to be overly emotional, out of control, unhappy, and even frightening. Anger is commonly recognized as a form of rejection; it shows that the angry person is narrow minded, not "laid back" or "free spirited." Like aggression, anger has no place in polite society.

The rejection of aggression as a human impulse has been so generalized that there are few circumstances and places in which it is considered acceptable. Nevertheless, it is a protective response; its purpose is to protect one from external threats, generally of a physical nature. It has been called the "instinct of self-preservation." In our time, apparently, the personal Self needs to be preserved only under those extraordinary circumstances when one's person or property is directly threatened. Few of us have a conception of an inner integrity that needs to be protected by the same instinct that protects our persons or wallets. We find ourselves, consequently, in a collective (social) environment in which this basic instinctual content cannot be directly expressed.

In the early days of an infatuation, aggression is expressed in the form of fears and fantasies that are then directed at one's self. When making love, lovers may call upon each other to "make it hurt" or to "do it hard." At face value these phrases do not express "what I want to do to you." Rather, they are expressions of aggression turned back upon oneself and they assure us that we are connected to the lover. The most obvious forms of aggression, of course, are real or fantasied rape and sado-masochistic acts. Indeed, fantasy plays a highly important role in discharging much of the aggressive impulses that are activated in infatuations, whether sexuality is actualized or not.

During infatuation aggression generally arises in a mutually acceptable form, either direct or indirect, and focused either upon oneself or the world. Mutually acceptable aggression, such as in love-making, is not regarded as aggression at all, but as an expression of one's self-confidence or fundamental lack of inhibitions. At such times it is not viewed as negative content but as an expression of personal development.

During an infatuation, aggression also may show up in another form; that is, it may be displaced onto others. When the preoccupation with a relationship becomes so great that one loses the ability to concentrate on the daily routines of life, one may become irritable and irritating. For example, Fred was normally an even-tempered, deliberate manager, but when he fell in love with Cindy the demanding details of his job made him impatient with and critical of his co-workers. On a day he had a minor setback in his plans with Cindy, his secretary happened to make a mistake which he caught, thereupon he lost his temper and loosed his aggression on her. This kind of behavior is symptomatic of the activation of instinctual drives in the early stages of a relationship.

SPIRIT

To understand love and infatuation, it is important to start by recognizing that they draw upon not only emotion, but also many subtle components of the psyche or personality. The psyche, described in some detail in Chapter III, is a totality, a continuum we may say, of constant activity at different levels of consciousness and unconsciousness, whether one is asleep or awake. Some activities and their sources can be identified to some extent and have been appropriately named, but others are so subtle yet pervasive we can refer to them only generally. Thus, the subtle activities that at one level of the psyche contribute to the numinous qualities of love and infatuation are part of what I call, generally, "Spirit." Because it is so intrinsic to our concerns, we must try to focus more sharply on it.

The complexity of the idea of "spirit" is reflected in the four pages devoted to its definition and usages in the *Oxford English Dictionary*. They can be summarized briefly here according to its two primary aspects and the short definitions given in other works.

The first aspect of "spirit" is defined succinctly in the *American Heritage Dictionary* as "the vital principle or animating force traditionally believed to be within living beings." This definition can be amplified by its accepted synonyms: anima, animus, atman (Hindu), pneuma, psyche, soul, and vitality; breath or essence of life, divine spark, *élan vital*, life force, and vital force (*Roget's Thesaurus*). I like to use the term "essential spirit" to encompass this first aspect of spirit, and I use it in the remainder of this work. It is integral to love and infatuation.

The second aspect is better understood by the definition provided in *Roget's Thesaurus*: "A prevailing quality as of thought, behavior, or attitude." The synonym for this definition is "temper," as in "the temper of the assembly." We can further elaborate on this meaning by adding the word "prevailing," as in "prevailing spirit." This latter term falls within the meaning of the German word *Zeitgeist*, "spirit of the times."

The two aspects of spirit are unified by their common characteristic: the quality of transcendence. By "transcendence" I mean the experience, whether internal or environmental, of something that is beyond the ordinary limits of experience, yet is personal in nature and puts one in contact with the transpersonal, either the god of laws or the god of love. However, even in transcendence there is a difference between the two aspects of spirit.

The prevailing spirit, or *Zeitgeist*, is a personal and/or cultural force that functions whenever we have an inner impulse or imperative that conflicts with what we have learned in our homes, schools, communities, or past experiences—the rules by which we adapt to ourselves and our culture (e.g., "Children should be seen and not heard"). In making these adaptations, we transcend our inner impulse or imperative and conform to the expectations of the people, institutions, and community that have influenced us. In other words, we accept the rules of others instead of our natures, and thus come in contact with the god of laws. If we violate these rules we feel guilty and even ashamed.

Adaptation exacts a toll. It requires us to stifle natural inclinations; that is, to alienate ourselves from what is natural in us. The degree of our alienation depends upon the extent of the adaptations we feel impelled to make. It was to just this problem that Freud dedicated himself when he observed how a fundamental drive in women, namely sexuality, was repressed by the cultural *Zeitgeist* of Vienna and produced the variety of neuroses which he studied and treated. Puritanical Christian dogma relating to sexuality is a classic example of a cultural prevailing spirit, and the experience of one's own puritanism exemplifies how we identify with the precepts that transcend our personal natures. Prevailing spirit takes many forms, and is anti-nature by definition. I constantly see evidence of this in my clinical practice.

Prevailing spirit plays a large role in creating intrapsychic and interpersonal conflicts; it is a concept with which we all can identify. Furthermore, examination of this prevailing spirit gives us a clearer picture, on both intellectual and feeling levels, of its difference from the first aspect of spirit—what I have labeled "essential spirit." The prevailing spirit tends to conflict with our nature and is experienced most forcefully when our nature is activated by internal or external stimuli. Our essential spirit, on the other hand, accords with our nature; it connects with what is most human in all of us.[3]

It is the connection to what is most human in us that characterizes the transcendent quality of an experience. The appreciation of art, for example, a painting by DaVinci or Picasso, puts us in touch with the universal experience of beauty and creativity. The transcendent experience of "born again" Christians brings them into direct contact with religious needs hidden deep within their psyches. Whenever we are touched by the essential spirit, we are animated, "re-created," and even awe-inspired by the wonder and (sometimes) the fearfulness of the world. The essential spirit in each of us connects us with the universal, and it is the latter that brings many of us into contact with God.

The following example of the relation between essential and prevailing spirit may be enlightening; it was provided by a couple during therapy. Their two children were aged four and seven at the time of the occurrence.

The two children were taken to Lake Zurich at dusk on August 1 to view a fireworks display. The viewing point chosen was a cliff on the west shore overlooking the lake; across from the cliff was a low mountain. Just as the father opened the car door and the children stepped out, a full moon began its rapid rise over the crest. The children watched with awe. They were still in that egocentric period when they considered everything to be at their command, or at least related to them. Thus, they were certain that their arrival had produced the magic that caused the moon to rise. For the first time, an experience brought the children into contact with the cosmos in an innocent and awesome manner, and they felt God within them. They were imbued with the universal sense of curiosity and wonder about the world and its natural phenomena.

For several days afterwards, the children tried to recapture the inspiring experience of that night. When they found themselves powerless to do so through the simple magic of their presence, they tried to recapture the experience through their behavior. They argued about the details of their arrival, what they had said and done, where they had sat, how they had stepped out of the car, and what they had worn. Despite their efforts, they could not duplicate the experience.

It is incidents such as this one that give rise to some rituals. For example, after experiencing the essential spirit and being unable to recreate it, some people would believe that they had done something wrong—had sinned—and therefore were unworthy of God's grace and presence. They would not give up hope, however; thus, they would try to reestablish the conditions of the awesome event by creating a dogma of rules to govern their behaviors. The dogma would become the prevailing spirit and substitute for the essential spirit. In other words,

the prevailing spirit would become the artificial recreation of the spontaneous connection with God.

When the prevailing spirit becomes the substitute for essential spirit,
it attempts to codify what seems to be true and universal in the world.
Although it may interfere with openness to one's essential spirit, prevailing spirit plays an important social role; it enables society to function
with relative smoothness by setting standards for individual and collective behaviors. Where an individual's most wonderful moments may
be the experience of his or her essential spirit, a society's best periods
are those in which everyone lives according to the prevailing spirit. At
its worst, prevailing spirit is anti-natural and tries to force individuals
to repress their natural inclinations. At its best, prevailing spirit is
structured to enhance the natural aspects of the personality and to
prevent dangerous conflicts between and among individuals.

At the deepest level, it is important to recognize that adaptations are
always made out of fear of abandonment, whether by a parent, a loved
one, friends, or a community. A person who is aware of his own power
and authority and of his right to be part of a family or group can choose
to make a sacrifice, but he need not try to protect himself by using
efforts contrary to his nature to please another person or persons. When
adaptation is the abandonment of one's nature in order to hold onto the
person one loves, one narrows the limits within which the possibilities
of one's personality can be expressed. Thus, over a period of time one
would lose contact with the animating life force of the inner creative
child, the child that permits us to look upon the world at times with
wonder and awe.

The role of essential spirit in a relationship is so inextricably connected to feeling and instinct that it is very difficult to separate them.
Lacking substance, essential spirit moves through and around lovers,
reflecting their innermost feelings and deepest instinctual needs. How
does spirit function? A crude analogy is an aerosol can. The container
holds two substances, one active, the other inert. The inert content is
the hair spray or shaving cream or whipped cream, and the active
ingredient is the propellant that forces the usable contents out of the
can. Likewise, in love the body contains the instinct and feeling which
can be brought into use only by the active agent, essential spirit.

Essential spirit, the expression of a person's most intimate needs and
desires, has a moving and transformative effect on lovers. Each is
influenced by the positive atmosphere created by the essential spirit
unleashed in and through the other. A marriage of essential spirits is
thus consummated, as is a union of the individuals' instincts and feeling.

The union gives birth to a third entity, the relationship, which is the offspring of the partners and yet belongs to neither. This offspring is as much an expression of the union as a child would be. Like the child who depends upon its parents for life, the relationship depends upon the essential spirit of each partner to survive.

The analogy to the child can be taken a step further. The two lovers nurture the relationship emotionally and physically in the same way that parents give food and love and attention to their new-born. The precious relationship possesses a fragile life which must be given sustenance; it is affected by the two lovers, and in turn affects them.

The effect of the relationship on the lovers is frequently noted by their friends. For example, Dale, a shy, withdrawn man, fell in love with Marie, an extraverted and active woman. Until then, Dale's free time had been spent reading or playing chess with a male friend, whereas Marie had spent her free time attending political meetings and sports events and socializing with her many friends. Marie and Dale met accidentally, and although they apparently had nothing in common, something they could not identify or understand drew them together. They went to films and read books together and enjoyed arguing about the works from their different perspectives.

The essential spirit in the relationship grew out of the excitement each felt at being with the other and sharing their different outlooks on life, feelings, and thoughts. Their conflict, debates, and shared love of words bound them in a way that seemed strange to people who knew them well. The relationship, and the spirit activated in them by the relationship, fulfilled a longing in each for just this kind of union. Neither determined the nature of this relationship; it grew out of the idiosyncracies of each and created the third entity—the spirit of the relationship—that was rewarding to both. In sum, the spirit of the relationship expressed the unconscious and not-yet-lived parts of their personalities that were activated by each other's spirit.

When one thinks about the tension involved in the early stages of a relationship, when the instinctual and feeling contents of each lover are activated, it is evident that a spiritual tension is also activated. As it emerges, it encourages a newness in one's outlook on and feelings about the world, especially in relation to the beloved. A certain dreaminess develops, sustained by fantasies as well as by the withdrawal of energy from those pursuits that once were but are no longer fulfilling. One may have found no meaning in or purpose to life prior to falling in love, yet that apathy vanishes as the lover and the love fill the present with both meaning and purpose. The fear of losing the beloved is at root a fear of losing the meaning of life so recently "discovered." This fear becomes associated with one's other psychic fears, and causes psychological tremors throughout one's personality.

Although conscious will and the pre-existing personality are held in abeyance by the unconscious during the early period of an infatuation, they begin to reassert themselves and to claim their former dominance in response to the tension, the agony, and the ecstasy of the burgeoning infatuation.

too bad.

NOTES

1. Feeling should not be confused with Jung's concept of "feeling function" which he defined as the rational evaluation of inner and outer stimuli.

2. Erich Fromm, *The Art of Loving*. New York: Bantam Books, 1967 (first published by Harper & Row in 1956), p. 30. Dr. Fromm (1934–1980), a German/American psychoanalyst, criticized Freud for "seeing in love exclusively the expression—or a sublimation—of the sexual instinct." (*Ibid*.)

3. Prevailing spirit and the psychological patriarchy form a continuum of control, especially in the lives of women, that bring many individuals into analysis and marriage counseling.

CHAPTER III

THE PSYCHE: STRUCTURE AND CONTENTS

> One's own self is well hidden from one's own
> self; of all mines of treasure, one's own is
> the last to be dug up.
> Nietzsche

> An unlearned carpenter of my acquaintance
> once said in my hearing: "There is very little
> difference between one man and another, but
> what there is is very important."
> William James

The personality is a complex amalgam of all the genetic, physiological, mental, experiential, emotional, psychological, interpersonal, and cultural influences that have befallen each of us during the course of our lives. They come together as contents of the unconscious, for the most part, and because they differ quantitatively as well as qualitatively in each person, each of us is unique. When the contents are required, they are strained through the integrants, attitudes, and functions—the key elements of the psyche (personality)—to form the individual's response to a particular person, place, or situation. Our unconscious contents, especially the integrants, become highly potent when we fall in love.

Each of us is a unique being, yet because we are human, we are alike. We are social animals and the products of the cultures in which we live; we are able to learn and to reason (although our reasoning powers may seem to diminish or to vanish when we fall in love); we have imaginations; we form emotional attachments; and we have feelings about ourselves, the world around us, and the people in that world. Each of us is born with the potential for an enormous repertoire of behaviors. We are not programmed for the behaviors as such at birth; what we are born with are predispositions *towards* certain behaviors. It is the difference between being born speaking English or Hindi or Spanish and being born with the genetic, aural, and structural capacity to learn the language, whatever it may be, of our environment. This means that most of us are predisposed to far more behaviors than we normally use; some of the behaviors that we seldom use are called up when we fall in love or have an awesome experience; or when we are faced with emergencies and we act without thinking; or when we find ourselves on the verge of committing a crime out of anger. If we seem to have something of Dr. Jekyll and Mr. Hyde in us, it is because we are so disposed, and the predispositions are integral to our psyches.

Mental health professionals tend to agree that large aspects of the personality develop out of the interaction of predispositions at birth and subsequent experiences. They do not agree, however, on the nature of the psyche and its component parts and on the role of heredity in personality theory. But the old nature-nurture battles are no longer being fought. Epidemiological studies of families with certain traits and the investigations of identical twins raised apart indicate that heredity plays a key role in our make up, and any arguments that may arise are over the percentages of influence attributable to heredity and environment.

— a rationale for learning from Lynchberg.

A Brief History of Depth Psychology

My purpose in this chapter is to present enough information on personality theory to provide a foundation for the discussions in the following chapters on how the psyche influences when and with whom we fall in and out of love. Thus I offer a brief survey of Freud's personality theory and of the developments in psychology, personality theory, and dream interpretation later contributed by C. G. Jung. The latter, who had been trained as a psychiatrist in Switzerland, became an associate of Freud's for a period when the ideas of the two men coincided but then Jung, who was almost twenty years younger than Freud and had many years of creative work ahead of him, went on to refine and elaborate his own ideas.

The outstanding contribution to psychology made by Freud is unquestionably the first cohesive and comprehensive theory of the unconscious and its relationship to mental disorders (he developed the theory with the help of Josef Breuer, an early colleague). The unconscious, generally speaking, was conceptualized by him as made up of whatever contents consciousness had rejected. All three components of Freud's psychic structure—the ego, superego, and id—have unconscious as well as conscious aspects. Essentially, he defined the ego as the function that reins in the impulses of the id because the ego consists, in part, of the "forces of civilization, religion, and ethics"[1] with which the id may conflict. The superego is supposed to be

> . . . the highest mental evolution attainable by man and consists of a precipitate of all prohibitions and inhibitions, all the rules of conduct which are impressed on the child by his parents and parental substitutes. The feeling of conscience depends altogether on the development of the superego.[2]

The id was described by Freud as the source of all elemental needs, as a chaotic substratum that contains the drives for physical nourishment, self-preservation, love, sexuality, and reproduction (preservation of the species). Humans are unlike other animal species in that women are not bound to an estrous cycle for sexual arousal. Indeed, for centuries in our history, women were regarded by religious leaders as unable to restrain their sexuality, and thus as the seducers of men. In the late nineteenth and early twentieth century in Vienna, when Freud was growing up and beginning his career in psychiatry, sexuality was considered a male domain. Sex was regarded "as an anarchical force which must be completely regulated by society."[3] Yet at the same time, in Austria as elsewhere in Western countries, the double standard was pervasive in sexual morality, and according to Stefan Zweig (an internationally known writer, one of Freud's contemporaries), Vienna was a "society . . . completely pre-occupied with the thought of sex."[4]

Jung, whom Freud had hailed as his successor in the early years of their association, also differed with Freud over the importance of sexuality, but not to the same extent as did Alfred Adler, another former associate of Freud. Jung agreed that sexuality plays a major role in neurotic symptom formation for many people, but he could not agree that it was the *only* actor and drive. Later he also argued that Freud's insistence upon attributing sexual connotations to such behaviors as an infant's suckling and toilet training was excessive. As far as Jung was concerned, Freud's psychoanalytic theory was a hypothesis, and as such was properly the beginning of research in psychology, not the conclusion. In the face of Freud's certain disapproval, Jung read the paper he had written on his particular conception of the unconscious to the Psycho-Analytic Society and then resigned from both the organization and his office (the presidency).

To Freud, the unconscious was a dark and threatening substratum of the psyche in which unadapted and maladapted contents lurked. Jung's clinical work, however, led him to conclude that although *some* unconscious contents meet Freud's definition, other contents possess great healing and creative capacities. Jung never denied the properties and processes of the unconscious that Freud had discovered and elucidated; indeed, Jung attributed them to what he called the personal unconscious. But he conceptualized another and more comprehensive and creative unconscious; the exploration and illumination of the psychic contents of this unconscious became his life's work.

Jung called the creative potential of this unconscious "collective" because it encompasses universal processes and possibilities for perception and action. In his researches in Greek and Latin sources, he found many similarities between the development, images, and motifs in the dreams, fantasies, intuitions, and insights recorded in those volumes and the development, images, and motifs his patients were bringing to him for analysis; these similarities led him to conclude that human beings have always had a common potential for perception and activity.

While working by himself and with both hospitalized and private patients, Jung observed that no one's personality is monolithic; rather, it is made up of a number of different aspects or sub-personalities that sometimes seem to be conflicting, yet each of which plays a part in maintaining the individual's psychic integrity. For example, we may seem to become a totally different, perhaps even an exciting, dashing person when we fall in love, and then, when the relationship leads to marriage or falters to an end, our old, sober personality takes over again. Or we may consider ourselves to be natural followers until an emergency arises and then, without thinking, we take the lead in meeting the crisis. In such instances, we are not manifesting multiple personalities (a pathological condition), but rather different aspects of ourselves. What holds all our different aspects together is the core of our psyches, the Self.

The Self

Jung approached his concepts of personality from the perspective of wellness or normality, not disturbance. He identified, at the heart of a person's psychic structure, a psychological entity that he termed the Self. This Self, he said, is not only the central point of the personality, but also the totality of psychic phenomena in the individual. Everything we are and do arises from the Self. Because each of us has a Self, we are like all other people in the world, but at the same time, because the Self in each person is unique, we differ from one another.

Usually we are not aware of the Self within us, but it is possible to experience it *directly*, in an infatuation or other numinous experience (i.e., as inspiration and animation or as an intimate connection with the divine or the cosmic), or *indirectly*, through dreams or conscious knowledge which has been gained from experience or reflection.

Because the Self is the reference point for all psychic events as well as the immutable and constant part of the personality, everything we experience belongs to the Self and is the expression of the Self. It is what differentiates us from other people, even from siblings with whom we have grown up in the same house and under the same conditions. Although our siblings may be fairly close to us in age and all the children in the family have been treated similarly by our parents, we still may have entirely different personalities. However much alike the stimuli to which we were exposed may have been, we experienced and responded to them in different ways because of the unique Self that shaped our reactions according to the Self's unique properties.

Given that all psychic activity belongs to the Self, and that psychic activity includes conflict as well as harmony, then it follows that the Self must be capable of being in opposition to itself. Indeed, the constant conflict in the Self is the source of psychic energy. Our capability for opposition of the Self to itself is illustrated daily in consulting rooms.

Bob, for example, had been hurt by and responded with instinctive anger to a careless action by Sally, with whom he was in love. At the session following the event, he felt a conflict between having made that instinctive response and his fear, also an instinctive content, that she might break off their relationship.

Another example of conflict in the Self takes us into the realm of psychic adaptations. In the course of his study of personality, Jung discovered a developmental stage in adulthood that no one had recognized previously. In psychoanalysis, the stages of development are related to sexuality. Jung's discovery was more comprehensive. He saw life as composed of two parts, each with a major psychological task. During the first half of life the major task is to adapt to the world (i.e., to became socialized and educated) and to make one's way (i.e., to start a career, marry, establish a family) in the world. In the second half, the task is to find meaning and balance and perspective in one's life. During this period the psyche calls upon the individual to adapt to her or his inner nature and to integrate those parts of the personality that were previously repressed or were never conscious. We see the activation of this stage in what has come to be known popularly as the "mid-life crisis." It is the period when the major conflict arises between inner and outer adaptations and the Self is in opposition to itself, sometimes to such a degree that it triggers dissatisfaction with one's life and a state of depression.

A third example completes this discussion of conflicts within the Self (I am spending so much time on the topic because it is at the root of many problems experienced in relationships). Ellen had learned during her upbringing that it is very important to be practical, so she always set practical goals for herself. During her college years, however, she discovered that she possessed considerable creativity in and talent for acting. Yet her upbringing led her to choose against a vocation in the theater. In her case, the internal conflict was between her creativity and what she regarded as the need to adopt a practical career goal.

Practicality is valuable because it can help one to avoid hardship. The danger in seeking a career in the theater is the potential for hardship. When Ellen chose to ignore or give up her aptitude for acting, she affirmed a value that was prized and taught by her parents. In itself, the value was not bad or abusive, but it did violence to her nature. This internal conflict brought Ellen to my consulting room.

The problem was not insoluble. Indeed, had she lived longer with the conflict between the need to be practical and her creative yearnings, she might have become aware of a new perspective, one that encouraged the synthesis of the conflicting opposites, to wit, that some needs can be met only if one is willing to take risks. This perspective is a product of the transcendent (reconciliation of opposites) function of the psyche. Experiencing it would have given Ellen the courage to face the dangers of her preferred career and to deal with whatever pain its pursuit may have incurred.

In Jung's conception, the unconscious has the capacity for creativity; the transcendent function is one example. When conflict is activated in the Self by inner and outer imperatives, the collective unconscious produces images that symbolize both sides of the conflict as well as possible solutions. These important images usually appear in dreams and fantasies, but they also may make themselves known as inspirations and major insights. When, in one's life, an opposition arises between beliefs and imperatives, choosing one and not the other can be very dangerous.

oh?!

In a relationship one is often confronted by a choice of agreeing or disagreeing with, for example, a loved person's particular request. In this situation, which is not at all unusual in an infatuation or marriage, the explicit question seems to be, "Should I do this or this?" There is also an implicit and more significant question: "What am I going to do in relation to that other person?" The first question ("This or this?") merely forces one to hang on to the conflict. The second question opens up other possibilities. It gives rise to a new image: "What do *I* want to do? What is in my nature to do?" Not, "What do I need to do to satisfy or to rebel against that person"; these latter alternatives would be acceding to what the other person—not oneself—wants and would leave one still rankling. The image of what is in one's nature to do is the work of the transcendent function. It is the intuitive expression of how to resolve the conflict creatively. When we assimilate a new perspective that has been generated by the transcendent function, we meet a product of reflection.

It would be very convenient at this point to be able to present a map of the psyche that would show the shape, size, and position of each integrant and its spatial relation to all the other integrants. A number of Jungian theorists have drawn personal conceptions of the psyche, but because of the amorphous nature of the subject, there probably are as many idiosyncratic differences in the illustrations as similarities. At the risk of being accused of oversimplification, I offer my own and perhaps equally idiosyncratic conception. My explanations include definitions of the integrants and their functions, and clinical examples that I hope will clarify the various processes and interrelations.

The Psyche

Figure 1 depicts the Self. Everything in the sketch is the Self, whether it is labeled "unconscious," "ego," "persona," "collective unconscious," "personal unconscious," or "Self." The Self can be metaphorized as a lake with a river running through it. All the contents of the lake belong to the Self, including the river, and the river represents something like the life process: the stream of life, so to speak. The ego is the Self's channel to consciousness. Another metaphor we can use to think about the Self is the sea. It is in constant motion, even when it seems to be placid; at other times, separate waves lift and crest and roll for long distances before they fall back, but however distinct they may appear they are still part of the sea and indistinguishable from it. We differentiate the integrants (so called because they indivisibly make

Persona:

1. Roles and expectations
2. Cultural ideals
3. Cultural images
4. Acceptable individuality

Consciousness:

1. Persona
2. Primary and auxiliary functions
3. Conscious attitude
4. Will
5. Known but private individuality
6. Known but unacceptable individuality

Ego:

Reference point for all contents of consciousness and receiver of contents of the Self being made conscious.

Personal Unconscious (Shadow):

1. Repressed personality traits
2. Repressed drives and instincts
3. Repressed memories
4. Repressed personal conflicts
5. Inferior function
6. Opposite attitude
7. Personal contents of complexes

Self:

Center and totality of all psychic processes. The totality of the individual's traits, capacities, and abilities. The final reference point.

Collective Unconscious:

1. Archetypes and archetypal cores of
   complexes, e.g., mother, father,
   individuation process
2. Instincts: sex, aggression and relationship
3. Psychic energy

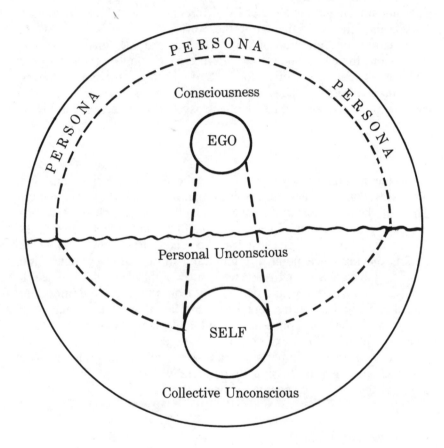

up the whole) of the psyche in order to be able to talk about specific functions and processes of the Self conveniently, not because the Self is a psychological patchwork. There are no seams in the psyche.

With the understanding that the Self is the center and totality of the psyche, let us first look at our "map" as a whole and then go on to discuss some of its major integrants. I shall try to avoid repeating myself, but reiteration is unavoidable when it is important to know how the same information is affected by different contexts. First, then, let's look at the relation of the ego to the Self.

In Jung's conception of the psyche, which provides the basis of our discussion, the ego is the center and reference point of *consciousness* and has an axial connection to the Self. That is, the ego's primary function is to serve as the reference point for those contents of the Self that are made conscious through inner (psychic) and outer experiences.

Self

As the totality of psychic activity, the Self is all the traits and processes, conscious and unconscious, manifested by one's personality. Thus, all the integrants of the psyche as well as the complexes, psychological types, functions and attitudes, instincts, and archetypes express the totality of the Self. Because it is the center of psychic activity, the Self is the reference point differentiating those traits, contents, and processes that are immutable and necessary for the psychological health and well-being of the whole personality from those that are important for adaptive and protective purposes, and lastly from those that pave one's way in the world but whose importance does not go beyond their adaptive qualities. An example of the latter trait is the quality of "niceness"; it may be important as an adaptive mechanism to enhance one's advancement professionally or socially, but it is of little significance in the larger perspective of one's life.

Collective Unconscious

Jung's major contribution to personality theory, the idea of the collective unconscious, encompasses the realm of the archetypes, complexes, and instincts which order the world and give us the potential for differentiating what is unique in us from what is present and fundamental in all human beings. We have access to the contents of the collective unconscious through integrants, dreams, day dreams, fantasies, and imagination.

The archetypes described by Jung are somewhat difficult to understand because they are only apprehended in images or by experience. Some psychotherapists and analysts disagree about the nature—even the existence—of archetypes, although scholars in other fields employ related concepts.[5]

In its simplest form, an archetype is an organizing property in the psyche. It acts as a magnet to draw experiences from the world and integrate them. Its purpose seems to be to order one's internal and external experiences and to integrate them within the psyche. For example, it is obvious that human beings have the capability to consciously differentiate female from male beings without looking at genitalia. We may say, then, that there is an archetype of the masculine and feminine that takes information from the world, differentiates it, and integrates it into the psyche. In this chapter, we shall look at only three archetypes: the anima and animus, duality or opposition, and individuation; they play important roles in infatuation and relationship. I shall also briefly describe complexes in which archetypes form the core. First, however, let us look at the collective unconscious as the repository of information about oneself and creativity.

The transcendent function, a creative aspect of the collective unconscious that has already been discussed, may be related to imagination and to the processes called up in the solution of scientific as well as personal problems. For example, P. B. Medawar, a Nobel Prize winner in medicine in 1960, rejected John Stuart Mill's belief in a "calculus of discovery" that leads a scientist from observations to truth in recognizable steps. Medawar holds that the act of generating new ideas is "the brainwave, inspiration or flash of imaginative insight that is the propounding of a hypothesis, a hypothesis being always an imaginative preconception of what the truth might be."[6]

> If the generative act in science is imaginative in character, only a failure of the imagination—a total inability to conceive what the solution of a problem *might* be—could bring scientific inquiry to a standstill. No such failure of the imagination—nor any failure of the nerve that might be responsible for it—has yet occurred in science and there is not the slightest reason to suppose that it will ever do so.[7]

We can infer from Medawar's observations that imagination is a fundamental human trait and that it is present in all of us to a greater or lesser degree.

Dreams are likewise a form of creativity in the unconscious. Robert Louis Stevenson, for example, the author of "The Strange Case of Dr. Jekyll and Mr. Hyde," wrote the story after its plot was revealed to him in a dream; he had spent years searching for a suitable story on the theme.[8] Jung also noted the storylike quality of dreams when he characterized them as "drama taking place on one's interior stage."[9]

Dreams have been assumed to have meaning since at least the beginning of recorded history, if not earlier. Two thousand years before the birth of Christ, Babylonians and Syrians were recounting and interpreting dreams, and a book on the meaning of different dream images was one of the first popular works published in Guttenberg's new movable type.

According to Ellenberger, "almost all the notions that were to be synthesized by Freud and by Jung" had been discovered between 1860 and 1899.[10] Both Freud and Jung agreed that dreams bring unconscious contents into consciousness but they differed on how the contents should be interpreted.

Mary Ann Mattoon, whose systematic presentation offers novices a step-by-step introduction to Jung's theory of dream interpretation, explains the reason for the importance given to the practice in analysis:

> A person's dreams yield information on how he views himself (his self-concept) . . . and on the relation between self-concept and behavior. [They also] provide access to the various levels of the psyche . . . and to the nature and causes of individual problems.[11]

Dreams are a door into the collective unconscious, and as such offer glimpses of the archetypes. The anima and animus archetypes, however, can also be experienced consciously, to some extent, in the individuals with whom we fall in love or in our images of what opposite-sex persons should be like. Essentially, the anima and animus archetypes are the psyche's capacity to differentiate masculine (animus) from feminine (anima). Moreover, the anima and animus archetypes are said to differentiate Logos (spirit and intellect) from Eros (relatedness or feeling).

Some theorists refer to the anima and animus as Logos and Eros in order to express their presumed qualities. Over the millennia, Logos has been associated with the masculine archetype, and Eros with the feminine. Logos means "word" and denotes structure; for example, God is "the Word," and has until recently been pictured as masculine. Eros, which takes its name from the god of love, is equated with love and relatedness.

Conflicts sometimes rage among analysts when they debate the question of the nature of the masculine and feminine archetypes. The argument always runs along familiar lines: on the one side is the contention that women's consciousness is naturally connected to Eros, and thus to relatedness, whereas men's consciousness is naturally connected to Logos, and thus to thinking. On the other side is the argument that women and men are acculturated, adapted, and coerced by the prevailing spirit to take on their respective "qualities." I have no desire to insinuate myself into the midst of this debate. I like to use the terms Eros and Logos to mean those qualities that have to do with relationship and intellect respectively, without regard to their attributed positions in the conscious economy of men and women.

Jung identified the anima as a female figure whose psychological *function*, in men, is to bring the contents of the unconscious to consciousness. He regarded the anima as the intermediary between male consciousness and the unconscious, yet connected to both. In a dream, the anima may appear, for example, as a beautiful woman introducing the fair-haired American dreamer to a swarthy European. The dreamer would represent the ego and the woman would be an anima figure introducing an unconscious character to the dream ego.

Just as Jung saw the anima as the feminine component in men, he saw the animus as the masculine component in women. The function of this character in a woman's psyche also seems to be mediatory. It is important to differentiate, at this stage, functional aspects of the anima and animus from their respective contents. We shall see shortly that the specific form (physical and character features of the anima/animus image in dreams) is taken from our everyday lives and experiences. The functional aspect of the anima and animus is not related to their image characteristics, but is concerned with the mediation of conscious and unconscious. In more concrete terms, a dream image of anima or animus must be interpreted from two different and complementary perspectives. The analyst will ask "What characteristics of this anima (animus) figure belong to you?" and "What parts of you does this anima (animus) figure lead you to confront?" The first question gets at the content of the anima or animus image; the second, at the unconscious contents being mediated by the functional aspect of the anima or animus.

The archetype of duality is *embodied* in the anima or animus. That is, all contents of the psyche possess dual or opposite natures: masculine–feminine, good–bad, and positive–negative, for example. In the psychic structure, ego is opposed by shadow, persona by the collective unconscious. By definition, duality does not mean conflict, although in most instances it is expressed as psychological conflict.

The individuation process is composed of a series of stages over which we have no control. In one stage, our own unconscious personality traits are projected onto the people in our lives who possess more or less similar traits. It should be kept in mind that projection is an unconscious activity that happens to us. In this stage we are led to react strongly, either positively or negatively, to this projection. The remaining stages of the individuation process result in the conscious integration of projections; that is, drawing those projections back to ourselves where they belong.

We shall see (Chapter IV) that the process of individuation leads to the projection of one's anima or animus onto the person with whom one falls in love, and that the duality fundamental to psychic activity plays a major role in the process of blackening or denigrating the marital relationship. Individuation thus requires the conscious integration of the projected traits in order to increase one's self-knowledge, and also to see others (including one's spouse) more clearly.

An archetype is also the core of a complex. It is important to understand the complex as a concept if we are to grasp the existence of individual differences among people. A complex is an amalgam of affects, attitudes, opinions, and experiences that have a common image—the archetype—at its core. One of the most significant characteristics of the complex is the large amount of emotion that is attached to it. For example, the old childhood saying, "Step on a crack, break my mother's back," sometimes becomes the magnet for a child's fears about abandonment and makes the child so fearful that he cannot walk normally along a sidewalk. Complexes may also be part of the shadow contents, which are associated with the personal unconscious (see the following section).

Complexes are formed during the course of our development when traits that belong to the personality are repressed because of our need to adapt to the environment and culture. For example, when lonely children create imaginary playmates, their parents often try to reason the children out of the fantasy or to ridicule the imaginary friends. If the parents succeed, it is not only the loss of the make-believe playmates that affects the children's development, but also the curtailing of their use of imagination. The more traits we need to repress as we develop, of course, the closer become the boundaries within which we feel safe to express ourselves. The consequence is a depression of psychic energy as well as a repression of traits, because it is our traits that animate our lives.

When we are living the lives that belong to us, that is, when we are free to express our natural traits, we are animated. When we must repress traits that are rightly ours, we live a collective life, not our own: we are dominated by the prevailing spirit of our families and/or cultures. The net result is a depression of psychic energy and the expression of ourselves within very clearly defined limits. Whenever this happens, there is a build-up in the unconscious of the energy due to the repression (use of energy to push from consciousness) of the so-called "unacceptable traits." The repressed content, of course, becomes part of a complex.

Shadow

The term "shadow" refers to those repressed personality traits that are part of one's personal unconscious. For example, in "The Strange Case of Dr. Jekyll and Mr. Hyde," the latter is the evil figure that appears after Dr. Jekyll ingests the transforming chemical. Mr. Hyde can be understood as Dr. Jekyll's shadow.

If we think of the ego as living in the full sunlight of consciousness, then the shadow lives in the ego's shade, in the obscurity of the unconscious, from which it intrudes upon infatuation, marriage, the break-up of marriages, and even our daily lives. As an example of the latter, consider an introverted man who works with a talkative and outgoing woman. He is greatly annoyed by these traits whenever he comes into contact with her, but many people in the office like her. When our introverted man called her this "insufferable" woman during a conversation with a friend, the latter pointed out that the complainer often becomes outgoing himself after he drinks a beer or two. "Yes," replied the complainer, "but I always feel so ashamed of myself afterwards. I feel that I have let the whole world in on my secrets!"

The shadow trait of this introverted man is extraversion, and obviously it is a source of embarrassment to him when it shows itself against his conscious will. He dislikes in his female co-worker the quality of extraversion that he himself possesses but does not value. Others see the trait in her as likable; to him it is "insufferable" because he sees in her what is, to him, insufferable in himself.

Anima/Animus

The anima/animus is one's contrasexual archetypal image.[12] This is not to say that we carry in our unconscious a specific picture of the kind of woman or man to whom we are drawn, but rather that the anima/animus predisposes us to recognize as desirable certain looks, attitudes, traits, behaviors, and mannerisms that we see in another person, and it is this recognition that makes the other person seem attractive and lovable to us.

In Latin, anima means "soul" and animus "spirit." Jung imagined the first to be the animating soul of men and the second, the inspiring spirit in women. We can see that Jung belonged with the proponents of Logos and Eros as natural conscious properties, respectively, of men and women.

There are, in a sense, two sides to the anima/animus image: the conscious and the unconscious. The conscious part relates to known and identifiable experiences of the opposite sex such as those that children and adolescents can describe and differentiate (e.g., the mother who tries to keep her son from engaging in "dangerous" sports; the father who calls his daughter "princess" and tries to fulfill her every wish). The consciousness of such patterns forms part of what we know about ourselves and our world. The other and larger part, so to speak, of the anima/animus consists of unconscious contents; they include all the repressed and never conscious aspects of our personality that deal with all significant images of and experiences with the opposite sex.

In early and middle childhood, anima content revolves around images of mother, aunts, sisters, and girlfriends; the animus content revolves around images of father, uncles, brothers, and boyfriends. At puberty and adolescence, when sexuality becomes a prominent part of our lives, the anima/animus takes on overt sexual contents.

The mother is a dominant image of the feminine. Experiences of the mother are organized around the archetype of the feminine, and the contents of all the mother-experiences form and become part of the mother complex. The same, of course, is true for the masculine archetype and the father complex. If the experiences of the mother and/or father are excessively anti-nature, then the corresponding complexes are one-sidedly negative in their properties. The mother and father complexes, however, not only comprise experience of the personal mother and father, but also of mothering and fathering experiences with other people in, and one's observations of, the world. Collective or cultural images and ideals of masculine and feminine and mother and father contribute to the contents of complexes and their functioning.

It is important here to observe the role of collective consciousness (persona) in perpetuating stereotypes of men and women. Historically, and down to the present, nature and the natural environment has been devalued and/or attributed to the world of women. We need only think of our attitudes toward sexuality, menstruation, jealousy, anger, need for relationship, and the like to be aware of the ways in which our prevailing spirit—our collective conscious ideals—have devalued these experiences and associated them so negatively with women. It is an impossible task at this moment in the development of human consciousness to differentiate what is in a woman's nature (aside from the biological, of course) from what is in a man's nature. In order to avoid stereotypes, therefore, let us agree to define Eros as relatedness and a problem for both men and women, given the devaluation of relatedness by our anti-natural prevailing spirit. And let us also, as I have done earlier, agree to use "prevailing spirit" and "essential spirit" to express the dual aspects of what has been called generally "Logos."

Throughout the rest of this book, we must understand the function of the masculine image of the animus. If the anima introduces a man to parts of his nature that are unconscious by repression or some other mechanism, we may say that, at least to some extent, it is directly attributable to the prevailing anti-nature spirit. The animus often appears in women's dreams as a man who leads the way to further understanding of her nature. I speculate that his function compensates the prevailing spirit, associated with the patriarchy, which has a decidedly anti-nature, anti-feminine attitude.

In the dream of one of my clients, the woman sees a dark man on a path that is, at first, parallel to hers. As they walk along, his path goes up and down and meanders right and left through a nature area. This animus character was demonstrating that life is not the shortest distance between two points, but is rather a serpentine path through nature.

To conclude this discussion, we can say that the anima introduces a man to his nature at a feeling level, while the animus provides a woman with an internal experience of her essential spirit. In the subsequent chapters we will see that a spouse becomes a confusing collage of mother or father, brother or sister, lover, colleague, or teacher. The unconscious mechanism of projection plays a central part in creating this proliferation of sometimes contradictory images.

The apparent "purpose" of infatuation is the projection of the anima/animus into the world (ie, onto the beloved), so that one may begin the painful and arduous task of reintegrating the projected contents. The remainder of this book deals directly with psychological processes as they manifest themselves in the process of falling in and out of love. We shall be able to see the uncanny similarity between Jung's alchemical studies and the psychological events that mark the progress of intimate relationships.

NOTES

1. A. A. Brill (Ed.) (1938). *The Basic Writings of Sigmund Freud*. New York: Random House (The Modern Library), p. 12.

2. *Ibid.*, Brill, pp. 12–13.

3. A. Janik and S. Toulmin. *Wittgenstein's Vienna*. New York: Simon & Schuster (A Touchstone Book), 1973, p. 47.

4. *Ibid.*, p. 46. Karl Kraus, one of the foremost editors, journalists, and satirists of the day, whom Janik and Toulmin cited as a "representative ethical spokesman for his milieu" (*Ibid.*, p. 10), listed hysteria as a major psychological problem afflicting the Viennese middle class and attributed its source to "the business character of bourgeois marriages. Marriages designed to create financial dynasties, regardless of the personal fulfillment of the parties guaranteed frustration, especially for women in so strait-laced a society. For the husbands, incompatibility meant recourse to prostitutes, or to affairs. . . . For the wives, the problem was more complicated, since it was instilled in them early on that only lascivious, depraved women could actually desire or enjoy sexual gratification" (*Ibid.*, p. 76). Many of Freud's patients were middle-class women suffering from hysteria.

5. For a discussion of the inferential supports of archetypes, see Mary Ann Mattoon (1981) *Jungian Psychology in Perspective*. New York: Free Press, pp. 42–45.

6. P.B. Medawar (1984). *The Limits of Science*. New York: Harper & Row, pp. 83–84.

7. *Ibid.*, p. 85.

8. M.A. Mattoon (1984). *Understanding Dreams*. Dallas, Texas: Spring Publications (originally published under title *Applied Dream Analysis: A Jungian Approach*, in 1978).

9. C.G. Jung, *Letters*, vol. 1; cited in Mattoon, *Ibid.*, p. 53.

10. H.E. Ellenberger (1970). *The Discovery of the Unconscious*. New York: Basic Books, p. 311.

11. M.A. Mattoon, *Ibid.*, p. 3.

12. The anima is the male contrasexual image, the animus, the female. Jung, being a male with a nineteenth-century upbringing, conceptualized the contrasexual image initially in terms of the masculine experience. Subsequently, he recognized the existence of a contrasexual image in females but gave it darker overtones than he attributed to the anima.

CHAPTER IV

INFATUATION: HOW WE ANIMATE

As we acquire more knowledge, things do
not become more comprehensible, but more
mysterious.
>
> Albert Schweitzer

There is no reality except the one contained
within us. That is why so many people live
such an unreal life. They take the images
outside them for reality and never allow
the world within to assert itself.
>
> Herman Hesse

For most of us, falling in love is one of the most moving experiences of our lives. It doesn't matter if we are rich or poor, young or old, cynics or realists—when we fall in love, we become more exciting to ourselves and others, and the world becomes a more exciting place. The *process* of falling in love is the same for all of us, which is why we all respond to similar visual or printed romantic plots.

One reason that falling in love is so wonderful is that we cannot choose to have the experience. It is something that happens—almost miraculously—*to* us. Nor can we choose with whom to fall in love. The element of chance is itself romantic. Some people say that opposites attract, yet there are no rules or formulas for falling in love with certain people rather than others. If we want to explore the issue, we have to look within ourselves.

We fall in love with a particular person (or image of a person) at a particular time because of the state of our psyche and the arousal of our anima or animus by that person. The arousal leads to the projection of the anima or animus onto that person. It is a simple process outwardly, but a very complicated one internally. The projection of the anima or animus induces a psychological and physiological condition in which all the integrants and other aspects of our personalities are involved. It is a condition that has little relation to our normal state. No woman would think of falling in love with a convicted murderer or rapist, yet time and time again we read reports in newspapers of women who have asked the courts for permission to marry such a person. What do they see in those men? Not the felons who have committed crimes, certainly, but personality traits that draw a response from each woman's psychic concept of the man she can love. What an unusual state is infatuation, to lead to such acts!

By definition, infatuation has been recognized throughout the ages as defying logic and even sanity. Samuel Johnson, for example, defined the verb "to infatuate" as "to strike with folly; to deprive of understanding." The current *Oxford English Dictionary* defines the adjective "infatuated" as "Made or become utterly foolish; possessed with an extravagantly foolish passion; besotted." And the *Random House Dictionary*, one of the better reference works on American English, follows the OED in defining the noun "infatuation," but adds the enlightening phrase, "all-absorbing passion." Whether inappropriate, short-lived, and ultimately regretted, or the beginning of a long, stable relationship, infatuation is indeed an all-absorbing state that brings one's psyche to new heights of feeling, imagination, and creativity. But it is more. Infatuation reanimates—freshens—the personality, and at the same time provides the energy to explore the mystery of the unique other person with whom one has fallen in love.

When our anima or animus opens the gateway to the animated world of infatuation, we are out of conscious control. Providing that we have no history of psychosis and are past the age of puberty, we see the person carrying the projection of our anima or animus as the beloved. It does not matter what are our origins, the languages we speak, or the traumas we have lived through—if our anima or animus is projected onto a particular person, we fall in love with him or her regardless of his or her skin color, eye shape, body build, intelligence, interests, or even response to us. Thus we may fall in love with unattainable others, such as film stars, teachers, or heroes; we usually speak of such incidents as "crushes" because of the fantasy elements they contain, but they are still infatuations. In other words, infatuation exists apart from time and taboos.

We must beware, however, of confusing infatuation with sexual arousal. The first is part of a creative process that involves the total psyche and proceeds to several other stages; the second is an instinctual reaction that is limited in scope and duration. Sexual arousal certainly occurs in infatuation, but infatuation is not essential to the arousal. What we examine in the following sections of this chapter is the process of infatuation in which sexual arousal and satisfaction occur as part of a process rather than as an end in itself.

Another Aspect of Sexuality

Introducing Mr. and Ms. Right has become a flourishing industry in the United States. Aside from libraries, night classes, church socials, and matchmaking friends—the traditional arenas for meeting eligible mates in our society—there are in most cities of any size now a host of profitable organizations and activities whose success is based on bringing people together and helping to alleviate their loneliness and desire for love. These may range from nontraditional newspapers in which individuals advertise their availability, to computer-dating agencies, rock concerts, singles bars and restaurants, and health clubs. They were brought into existence by the revolt against Puritanism that began in our society prior to World War I because of deep dissatisfaction with the traditional mores governing relationships in general and sexuality in particular. This is not to say that the revolt has ended; we are, I believe, still in the process of forging a new set of mores.

At the societal or collective level, four movements in Western culture after World War II speeded up the loosening of outmoded puritanical morality, namely the consumerism associated with postwar prosperity, anti-war (anti-establishment) activism, feminism (including the availability of uncomplicated birth control measures), and rock music. There have been other periods in Western history when comparable revolts occurred, for example, in the latter part of the first millennium and early parts of the second. The Protestant Reformation was also a time of cultural upheaval on a grand scale.

Lawrence Stone, author of the monumental study, *The Family, Sex and Marriage in England 1500–1800*,[1] traces several phases of sexual attitudes among the upper classes that were "more or less successfully imposed" upon other classes.

Moderate toleration: up until the last decades of the sixteenth century.
Repression: about 1570 to 1670.
Permissiveness ("even license"): from about 1670 to 1810.
Repression: 1770 to mid-Victorian period.
Permissiveness: 1970 to present (apogee in 1970s).

He attributed these oscillations to "cultural—and particularly religious—changes."

Both sexual repression and sexual permissiveness eventually generate extremist features, which in turn set in motion counterforces which by a process of "social reversion" slowly turn the pendulum back in the other direction. . . . There is no reason to believe that there is a cyclical law in operation, for the swings can be accounted for by specific changes in religious enthusiasm, and by the time it takes for excesses to generate their own opposites.[2]

It is important to realize that the oscillations are not identical. On the swings back, they do not go back as far, and on the swings forward they advance ahead of the old positions.

Social diseases (e.g., syphilis and gonorrhea) were rampant in Europe and England after the bacilla were transported from America, but they seem to have had no effect on sexual attitudes. If, as it seems possible, the United States currently is at the beginning of a swing to a more conservative sexual position, the reason may be an equal dosage of the fear of AIDS and the rising strength of conservative religious groups and their reaction against sexual license.

In each period, the common effect is the transformation of the consciousness of the larger culture by the questioning of and revolt against the conventional wisdom relating to religious principles, sexual mores, and personal relations. The major characteristic prior to each period of upheaval is the kind of psychic stagnation that precedes infatuation in an individual; that is, the need for renewal. In individuals, the need is met by the projection of the anima or animus upon a potential lover; in collective groups, the need is met by overthrowing the rigid prevailing spirit. In both individuals and the collective, consequently, creative energies are released. Thus our century's so-called "revolution" must be considered within the historical framework of other periods of foment, and seen as a psychological as well as political and religious (moral) struggle that occurs internally—in the microcosm—as well as externally—in the macrocosm. The consequences of the turmoil that we have been through in the United States are still evident.

Because sexual freedom was extolled in the 1960s, unhindered sexual activity became the ideal for large segments of the population. Freud spent much of his life studying the effects of repressed sexuality on the psychological states of his patients; today, psychologists and analysts may expend much of their efforts studying the effects on current clients of identification (either conscious or unconscious) with a sexual morality that provides no clear limitations. Just as Freud identified symptoms stemming from the repression of sexuality, modern social scientists find symptoms of over-expressed sexuality: rampant teen pregnancy, "addiction" to sexual activity, impotence, and genito-urinary diseases. The question, of course, is whether there are options other than repression or over-expression. When a sexual impulse arises, must it be gratified immediately? Is there anything we can do other than repress it or express it? This question is of particular relevance to infatuation.

The link between sexuality and essential spirit has been observed by many different peoples over time and has been extolled in poetry, discussed at great length in religious works, and made the focus of considerable art. In Asia, sexuality has been incorporated into the spiritual life of religion and in religious rituals. Even in the West, sexuality is often given a role in splinter religious movements to express the essential spirit within us.

The relevance of sexuality to infatuation is its potential for self-expression on the three levels described in Chapter III: instinct, feeling or relatedness, and spirit. The extent to which we are willing to risk expression of the deepest parts of ourselves in a sexual act is directly linked to the degree that we have integrated the three levels into our conscious personality. We are most sensitive to injury in connection with those parts of ourselves that are, at least to some extent, unconscious. Inasmuch as the integration of the three components of ourselves is entirely an individual matter, no universal morality, whether restrictive or permissive, can specify the struggle that occurs within each of us over our sexuality.

Perhaps looking at the role of sexuality in our lives in the context of a relationship will illustrate the conflict we go through more clearly. Jane, a 35-year-old woman, is unmarried but involved in a sexual relationship with Bob; the couple has agreed that their relationship will be an exclusive one. Jane wants to marry Bob, but he is unwilling for some very good reasons not specifically related to her (he has too many compulsive traits at present with which he must come to terms before he can commit himself to marriage).

From time to time, Jane tries to meet and date other men because marriage and children are of paramount importance to her. She is very conscious of the ticking of her biological clock. She wants either to end the relationship with Bob or marry him. Yet she cannot end the relationship because she regards it as a serious connection, even though it is expressed almost exclusively through their sexuality.

Jane and Bob see each other once or twice a week. They have entirely different interests. When they are together each assumes a facade (persona) in order to avoid the conflicts that are inherent in their natures and relationship. In fact, they talk very little with one another and seem unable to care about each other's daily struggles. Nevertheless, Jane regards theirs as an intimate relationship because they have sex. She has occasionally met other men she liked, but she cannot permit herself to start a sexual relationship with any of them given her commitment to Bob. Yet she was attracted to those other men.

When we examine Jane and Bob's situation, we see a problem typical of many contemporary couples. The sexual nature of the relationship reflects its "depth" because Jane "does not engage in casual sex"; however, she does not love Bob and he refuses to marry her. Their sexual couplings are instinctive and even at times spiritual (i.e., inspiring), but for Jane, at least, the sex act doesn't necessarily feel like a *union* with Bob; in short, her sexual expression is related to an animus lover she sees in Bob, but not to Bob himself.

Jane's feeling life is her most vulnerable area. She can be quite animated when she is with other people, but she has great difficulty relating to them as individuals. Thus her sexuality is a substitute, albeit an unconscious one, for relatedness. She cannot try to develop another relationship because for her it would have to be sexual and her pact with Bob forbids sex with anyone else. So she is stuck.

This scenario, with minor changes, is frequently recounted by men and women in many consulting rooms. When sexuality precedes relatedness it often becomes the substitute for and diversion from relatedness. I do not believe that sexuality should always come after relatedness, nor do I believe there is some magical answer to this dilemma. There is no psychological ideal, no universal psychological morality, that can be used as a guide for sexual behavior in all or even many situations. Another woman faced with Jane's inner conflict might resolve it by dumping Bob or by starting an affair with some other man to whom she is attracted. Jane behaves as she does because she is who she is, has experienced what she has experienced in her life, and repressed what she has repressed. Her relationship with Bob symbolizes the state of her personality.

There is no collective model or support system for true sexual freedom that has no ideal other than to express one's sexual nature and morality. We can learn this fact only by trial and error, by paying attention to the effects on our feelings and spiritual life of our sexual impulses, behaviors, and even failures to act.

We cannot fault Jane for the bind in which she finds herself. Nor can we fault all those men and women who have identified with an ideal, whether puritanical or libertine, and then have felt the pain of betraying their sexual natures. Given the power and intensity of sexuality and the many facets of its expression, it becomes a ready vehicle for carrying all of our feeling, instinctive, and spiritual natures. The weight of this pressure damages sexuality itself; it also keeps us from engaging the other possible vehicles (compassion, humor, playfulness, and quarreling) that relate us to other people and enable us to live our lives totally rather than one-sidedly.

At the risk of sounding too earnest, let me say that infatuation should not be regarded lightly. Arising as it does out of a stagnant psychic stage, an infatuation can carry us not only into an all-absorbing passion, but also into a period of intense creativity that permeates all aspects of our life. The consequences that follow such a period may have a lasting effect on our being.

The Preparatory Stage

Lovers often wonder why they were attracted to each other at that particular time and place. What made that particular evening or afternoon more enchanting than others? Was there some magic in that first glance? Was there something magical in the air? Was it something they did? Were they perhaps unconsciously looking for each other?

The answer is simple. One becomes infatuated with a person when one is in a psychic state of readiness for infatuation. Many of us have had the experience of trying to play matchmaker for two people who seemed eminently suited to each other only to watch them maintain a cold disinterest throughout the evening. Later, if we ask why, we get a shoulder shrug in reply or the excuse, "I wasn't in the mood, I guess," or "I was busy thinking about a problem at work." Nevertheless, if the same two people meet at another time, when they are psychically ready to fall in love, and if they "see" the image of a lover in the other, then the attraction will be almost magnetic. The key phrases here are "ready to fall in love" and "see the image of a lover in the other."

Despite Tennyson's poetic conceit that "In the spring a young man's fancy lightly turns to thoughts of love," readiness to fall in love is not seasonal. We become infatuated at any time and anywhere, providing that our psyche is in a receptive state. This is a psychological stage in which one is not especially active and does not feel especially attractive or lovable. It is a stage in which one seems to be in the doldrums: somewhat listless, perhaps mildly depressed, and low in spirit. The image that comes to mind is of a stagnant pool of murky water that just sits under the sun and appears to have no life. One seems to be going nowhere; nothing of interest is happening and it is difficult to build up enthusiasm about anything. One's life seems to be in a rut and there is little to look forward to. Yesterday's promises appear frayed at the edges and the landscape of the future stretches ahead bleakly. It is not that one has fulfilled all one's ambitions and has nothing to strive for, but rather that the joy has gone out of the striving. Everything seems stale and perhaps even futile. One feels as if life has been placed on "hold," and all one can do is to go through the motions automatically.

Months or even years later, if we look back on that period before we fell in love, we may recognize it as a state in which we had little conscious awareness, and little conscious awareness of our stagnation.

This dry-as-dust, unproductive stage, however, is when we are most vulnerable to falling in love with the person who approximates our unconscious ideal of a lover. With luck, we are in the right place at the right time to meet that person. This stage also can be the prelude to an intensely creative period in our life, since projection of the anima or animus taps the dormant possibilities of the unconscious.

The Infatuation

An infatuation starts when one's anima or animus is projected onto another person. This projection evokes a tremendous burst of physical and psychic animation that inundates one's consciousness with unconscious contents. The reason is that the animation stemming from the projected anima or animus also lowers one's level of consciousness (*l'abaissement du niveau mental*). The term refers to the weakening of the barriers that insulate one's consciousness from unconscious contents, which results in the flooding of consciousness by psychic energy, desires, and impulses that heretofore were unconscious. Thus the ego is overwhelmed by unconscious contents, and we find ourselves in a kind of twilight state. Time and other orienting factors, including our prevailing spirit, become somewhat confused and we begin to live out those psychic contents that had been repressed but are now energized. The apparent purpose of the lowering of the level of consciousness is to allow us to reintegrate traits that are in our nature but, for one reason or another, have been repressed because we could not accept them consciously.

We must keep in mind that every behavior, thought, and feeling experienced as part of an infatuation must ultimately be attributed to the projection of the anima or animus onto the person of the beloved. All the other factors examined in the rest of this chapter arise out of and are consequential to the projection of the anima or animus. The meaning of the projection of this contrasexual integrant, therefore, must be carefully examined in order to establish a firm grounding for our understanding of why we fall in and out of love with a particular person.

We have assumed up to this point that infatuation occurs simultaneously in each partner. In Chapter V (and particularly Endnote 7, in which the myth of Atalanta and Hippomenes is discussed), we shall see that the act of wooing or courtship plays a great part in the excitement and tension of infatuation. Biologically, courtship is a necessary prelude to copulation in all species. The nature programs shown on public television, for example, spend considerable footage showing the courtship rituals of different species. In the lower animal kingdom, males inevitably initiate the rituals. Until comparatively recently, the same thing was true among humans: courtship was generally initiated and conducted by men, which meant that a woman was limited in the selection of a sexual or marriage partner to those men who showed a preference for her. Nevertheless, there always have been women who have subtly or openly "chased" after men. More and more women in recent years are acting on their animus-projections to pursue men of their own choice. This practice is still not widespread, however, because of the dictate of the prevailing spirit which assigns men the role of aggressors in love.

We know that infatuation starts with the projection of our anima or animus upon a person of the opposite sex. At that moment we are caught. It is the moment when "time stands still"; when the other becomes the focus of the world; when one suddenly feels a surge of wondrous power within. This is the fascination that poets and songwriters have immortalized in the "I-took-one-look-at-you-and-can't-get-you-out-of-my-mind" theme. It doesn't matter whether the object of one's fascination feels a complementary attraction at once or not. When one is infatuated, one is virtually driven by the animus/anima to court the other. And what is courtship but the attempt to awaken the love object's anima or animus so that it will be projected onto the wooer and lead to the excitement, delights, joys, agonies, and creativity of mutual infatuation?

Before the infatuation becomes mutual, we can describe the plight of the wooer as suffering from unrequited love, a state in which there is an emotional, spiritual, and instinctual gap between the infatuated person and the other. It is a painful state, because the spurned lover experiences all the feelings and affects described in Chapter II, but with exaggerated loneliness and increasing tension, perhaps even to the point where his feelings are expressed in an aggressive manner.

Although more prevalent in adolescent infatuation, hostility in the face of one's own infatuated feelings is not unheard of among adults also. For example, a male analysand of mine recently had been telling me of his strong attraction to a female colleague. They had talked on numerous occasions; she smiled often at him, and he at her. He asked her advice on certain matters, all connected to his "courting" behavior. His "plan" was to ask her to lunch some day, as if it were a spontaneous thought on his part. The problem: she brought her lunch to work every day. One day, he saw her scrounging through the refrigerator in their lunch room and my analysand, in utter frustration, made some bitterly sarcastic remark about her search for her "brown bag." Needless to say, his later apology served equally well as an opening to a lunch date.

The foregoing brings up another area of infatuation that is self-evident and yet has far-ranging consequences. When our anima or animus is awakened and projected onto an unresponsive other, we have to find ways of making the other "see" us. Certain fowls conduct elaborate courtship dances for this purpose, insects send out plaintive twitterings, and some animals put on fearsome displays of aggression. Such behaviors are termed "natural." Comparable behaviors in human beings probably would be termed "manipulative," although in fact they may be just as instinctive as the mating dances, calls, and contests of other species.

I am not saying that all courtship behaviors are instinctual, although our instincts probably are surprisingly influential. Rather, I would call the "chase"—our efforts to win the object of our infatuation—a plot or drama as unavoidable as is infatuation, because the things we do to be noticed and desired stem from our unconscious. What we are unconscious of are the interplay and conflict between ego, anima/animus, and shadow, the mother lode of psychic material that is mined during an infatuation. These integrants are discussed in Chapter III, but we look at them again later in this section.

If courtship or the chase is about making ourselves attractive to the other, then obviously the persona plays some part in the process, and the ego an even more important one. The ego is identified with the energy, self-confidence, and self-absorption evoked by the activation of the anima/animus. The persona, however, is what we want to show the other; it is "contained," "protected," "given strength" by the energy and Self-connection generated by our activated anima/animus. We feel "full of ourself" and confident of our value. If we try to strut or act alluring, behaviors that we probably would not dare to risk at another time, it is because our anima/animus encourages us to do so. The fact that we engage in behaviors during infatuation that are not normal to us is what gives rise later, when our equilibrium is restored, to the charge of manipulation. This is not to deny the existence of people who consciously try to arouse feelings of love in others solely for purposes of exploitation or personal gain of whatever kind.

The chase culminates in the capture, that is, in the awakening of the anima/animus in the love object, and in the mutual experience of infatuation described in Chapter II. To be captured is "to be hooked." The love object is now animated and fascinated by the "image" of the chaser, the "image" being a combination of persona traits that are encouraged, energized, and protected by the activated anima/animus. The persona during the chase is real; it has substance and roots deep in the personality because it is energized by the anima/animus, and by extension, the Self.

I have switched from using the term "courtship" to "chase" and "capture" because power is expressed by the latter terms, and in infatuations the will to power is present in both partners. In fact, the woman's dream series presented in Chapter V shows as much "chase" and "capture" as the dreams of some of my infatuated male analysands. The conflict between love and power arises the moment that the anima/animus of the love object is activated.

The conflict between power, the impulse to "capture" the beloved, and love—the desire to interrelate with her or him—is the expression of the interplay between ego, anima/animus, and shadow. Thus we can see that shadow contents are subject, at the moment of repression, to the use of power—we use our energy to divert attention away from the unacceptable trait or feeling through any of our defense mechanisms, until finally we forget it belongs to us in the way we first perceived it. With the activation of the anima/animus, shadow contents are also awakened, in the form of urges, feelings, memories, fantasies; positive traits will often be repressed and so become a part of the shadow. We repress them not because we think they are bad but because we associate them with other behaviors and traits we find unacceptable. Many men will say that they are uncomfortable dancing to modern music. They do not judge this type of dancing as bad; they may even envy men who are adept. Yet for many men the discomfort about dancing centers around another shadow conflict. Men in our culture are often directly or indirectly taught to be circumspect and unemotional. Modern dance is neither circumspect nor unemotional. Hence the inhibition, and with it stagnation in the emotional realm. When a man's emotional life is activated in an infatuation, dancing may be a positive by-product. The old inhibition is consciously contrasted with the liberation of the infatuation. The liberation is associated with the beloved, and in the case of our imaginary man, capturing "her" is synonymous with "capturing" the emotional part of himself.

All of this is a preface to the assertion that infatuation is the expression of power in conflict with the desire to relate with love. By trying to "capture" the positive traits and feelings we "see" in the beloved, we are trying to integrate them into our everyday life. There are two inherent problems with this, however. First, the beloved is not only those traits and feelings we see, but a whole lot more that we have *not* yet seen. We literally reduce our beloved during infatuation to only those traits that are projections of ourselves. Second, while the shadow traits and feelings remain projected they are impossible to integrate, and so we depend on the beloved remaining unknown to us in order to maintain the projection. If the beloved comes out from behind the curtain of projection, that is, if she demands to be seen as different from his "image," she creates a dissonance in his perception—a psychic conflict—that can be resolved only in one of three ways: first, true integration of the shadow content; second, repression of his *reaction* to seeing the beloved as herself (that is, denying the reality of his perceptions and emotional reactions); or third, trying to exert control over the beloved by any of a number of means, for example, anger, disapproval, withdrawal, pouting, and the like.

The dissonance and the reaction to it arises inevitably as the encounter between lover and beloved deepens. The dissonance arises at what I call "the magic moment," not because it is so pleasant, but because it produces such profound changes in the relationship.

Let's take an extreme example from the typical exaggerations of today's television dramas that are fascinated with psychopaths, because they illustrate power, love, and "the magic moment." Here comes the psychopath who, through some twist of fate, has fallen in love, but at a distance, with a beautiful and vulnerable woman. He watches her; he stalks her; he fantasizes about her; and he imagines her personality, her feelings, her kindness, and her gentleness. Then one day, he stands next to her at a newspaper kiosk. He cannot take his eyes from her. She glances at him in the same way she looks at all strangers. Because he does not look away, she gives him a quick, polite smile, and leaves to go about her business. As far as she is concerned, he no longer exists. He, however, interprets her neutral behavior as the rejection of him as a man. Obviously, she is not so pure as he had fantasized; she is, instead, like his mother, a rejecting and abandoning "bitch." His fascination consequently turns to hate, and he stalks her to kill her. Dramatic, isn't it?

In our more everyday infatuations, in which there is a mutuality of interest and fascination, the "magic moment" comes for each lover when he or she makes an accommodation to the other out of fear of rejection and abandonment rather than out of genuine love or compassion or relatedness to the need of the other. In Chapter V we shall see the psychological prelude to the "magic moment" and then its effects on the relationship. In passing, however, we can say at this juncture that the "magic moment" brings the "parents" into the relationship, and with the "parents" comes power. And with power comes the need to repress our own desires and traits, control the desires and traits of our beloved, and finally, but much later perhaps, to suffer under the oppressive weight of a heavily regulated relationship, or alternatively, to feel hunger for the satisfaction of spiritual and emotional needs long ago repressed in the name of some idealized image of independence.

Anima/Animus

Projection is not a conscious act. It is a process that occurs without our volition or desire and whether we like it or not. In *The Golden Ass*, by the Latin writer Apuleius, the hero is turned into an ass because of the projection of his anima onto a maidservant and his consequent infatuation with her. His later struggle and encounter with the goddess Isis impels him to integrate women and his own feminine (anima) component into consciousness as a reality to be faced rather than an object to be seduced.

Anima and animus, when activated by projection, have the effect, as their common root indicates, of animating the conscious personality. All the psychic liveliness described in Chapter II and the awakening of one's creativity during infatuation result from the animation of the personality. The stagnation that precedes the projection of the anima or animus is a necessary antecedent to infatuation because it is symptomatic of a narrowing or limitation of the personality brought about by repression, of no longer being able to find meaning or satisfaction within the confines of our old ways of being and seeing things. In fairy tales or myths, this situation is symbolized by the old king (old prevailing spirit) who is weary and fragile and whose kingdom (the totality of the psyche or personality) has become unproductive. His people have become lethargic. Suddenly, a young, handsome hero, a prince, appears and rescues the king's daughter. He wins her hand by overcoming threatening obstacles and assumes the throne when the old king dies. The palace and the kingdom are restored (animated) to their former glory and all the subjects are released from their lethargy.

This myth is enacted again and again in our society; for example, when a married person falls in love with someone outside the marriage and is rejuvenated by the animation stemming from the projected anima or animus. Sometimes the marriage ends in divorce and sometimes the animation is turned back into the marriage. A married person also may become infatuated again with his or her partner when a dormant or new aspect of the anima or animus is projected onto the spouse and the resulting animation brings fresh life to the relationship. The awakening and projection of the anima or animus is the psyche's rebellion against the limits imposed on the personality when the ego's perspective has been narrowed through loss of its connection to the Self and the unconscious. Thus the projection of the anima or animus loosens the stranglehold of the one-sided ego perspective, causes a lowering of the level of consciousness, and brings about the direct experience of many personality traits that had been repressed or never conscious.

From the standpoint of the unconscious, we can liken the process to a rebellion led by a hero against a tyrannical ruler (the ego). In an infatuation, the hero, of course, is formed of the new possibilities created by the anima or animus after it has been projected onto the beloved; and it is this projection with the consequent lowering of the level of consciousness that saves us from dissatisfaction, loneliness, boredom, and stagnation.

The psyche has an impressive capacity to stimulate us when we are out of step with the Self. Unfortunately, in order to recognize the animation as a part of ourselves, we must first experience it as a projection onto another person. From our cultural perspective, love and relationship is not something inside us that flows to the object, but rather something that exists "in" or "because of" the object.

Imagine how different we would be if we said, instead, "It is my idiosyncracy that my love flows to her when I need to love." This statement seems staid, mechanical, and even "narcissistic"; yet it places the locus of feeling correctly with the person feeling it. We do not, however, in an infatuation, experience the feelings as arising "in" us, but as an extension of the beloved. Nevertheless, when the level of consciousness is lowered, we have immediate contact with traits, feelings, attitudes, and experiences within us, and perhaps even with people we had ignored or disliked before. Parts of ourself that were unconscious previously are activated and experienced "in" the beloved as a result of the projection of the anima or animus. Our sexuality, sense perceptions, intimacy, trust, energy, and other psychic components are experienced differently. A man, for example, who has been expressing his sexuality in a routine and uninteresting manner suddenly feels new powers and sexual hunger when he thinks about or is with the beloved woman (every part of ourself has both a conscious and unconscious element; thus while we are living out one part of our sexuality, we still may be inhibited about or unconscious of others).

The anima and animus are made up of the traits, attitudes, and behaviors we associate with specific people as well as the distillation of our experiences with them; when our anima or animus is projected onto an individual, then we find those same traits in the individual. Love is considered blind because we see, when we are infatuated, not the person upon whom we bestow our affections, but our image of what we expect the person to be. This distortion is created by the anima and animus. Thus we see that infatuation has two levels of activity.

First, the *conscious*: we see in the beloved traits that we have been conditioned to expect in people of the opposite sex. We may say that we have fallen in love with Mary or Andrew because she or he is kind, warm-hearted, giving, outgoing, and so forth. In fact, Mary or Andrew may have all these traits, but they are certainly not the only ones who do. We can conclude, therefore, that the traits in themselves are not the reason we fall in love. Consciously, we can try to rationalize why we fell in love with Mary or Andrew but we cannot *know* because consciousness has had nothing to do with fueling our infatuation.

Second, the *unconscious*: love is engendered at a deep level of the unconscious, in that part of the anima or animus of which we never have been conscious or which we have repressed out of consciousness. The activation of this stratum of the psyche provides the abundance of energy and interest that propels us out of our doldrums and into the relationship. But, as with the activation of any unconscious content, the experience is both pleasurable and painful. The pain is created by the sudden interjection in our lives of heretofore unconscious traits, feelings, impulses, wishes, attitudes, and opinions that seem alien and that we may even fear, since anima and animus have the psychic function of mediating between consciousness and the unconscious. Thus the activation and projection of the anima and animus also result in the projection of other unconscious contents, some of which may make us very uncomfortable. One way to understand the process is to imagine the anima and animus as introducing us, during infatuation, to parts of our psyche that we never knew before.

We may consciously believe during an infatuation that the beloved has taught us many things and made us aware of feelings and desires we had not known previously. In fact, however, the activation of the anima or animus made us receptive to the novelty of ourselves. Our unconscious and conscious experiences cannot be denied. In Chapter V, I present and discuss a series of dreams that clearly demonstrate how our unconscious and conscious experiences reflect and interact with each other. The dream series is similar in many respects to the dreams of other infatuated analysands. The dreams' contents and the dreamers' experiences contribute to a deeper understanding of infatuation for all of us.

The Shadow

By mediating between unconscious and conscious contents, the anima and animus mediate between the ego and the shadow. The latter is that part of the personality capable of being conscious, but repressed by the ego. By definition, the contents of the shadow contradict the traits valued by the ego. Sexuality, for instance, is an instinct and may also be part of the shadow contents activated by the anima and animus. By using sexuality as an example, we can see how the animus and anima activate a shadow trait in infatuation, making it accessible to the ego.

The activation of the anima and animus deposes—at least temporarily—the old narrow limitations imposed by one's ego and persona; the result is that conscious controls on parts of the personality are loosened. Ordinarily, the instinctive aspects of sexuality arise from the unconscious and are distilled through those consciously learned attitudes and ideals that are part of the ego's perspective. These attitudes and ideals become inoperative, however, in an infatuation, and the lovers are free to express their sexuality in whatever manner seems suitable to them at the time. A woman, for example, who has suffered the burdensome belief that sex is a duty owed to the husband by his wife, did not remember or believe this precept when she fell head over heels in love; rather, the activation of her instinctive sexual feelings freed her to engage in sex with her lover as an expression of their love for each other. Only later did the conflict arise between her old, burdensome ego standpoint and her animated feelings, when she remembered and felt the weight of her earlier attitude.

The conflict between ego and shadow is played out concretely in the form of fears of loss, abandonment, separation, and feelings of jealousy and resentment. In addition to the pleasant experiences of an infatuation, we feel tension and self-consciousness as well. Instinctive sexuality and the need for relationship are satisfied by the touching, talking, sharing, and expressing that are hallmarks of this state. But when the anima and animus are projected, shadow characteristics are also projected, not only onto the beloved but also into the world. Thus we begin to see vague images of threatening people or events which may have painful effects on the beloved and the relationship. The vague images are shadow characters and traits threatening to make themselves known to us. Although we shall see in Chapter Five how this works in a specific circumstance, it would be useful to give an example of the shadow threat. An introverted man becomes extraverted when he falls in love. Extraversion is for him a shadow characteristic. The man may or may not be able to hear the inner voice accusing him of being a silly extravert, but the voice is nevertheless felt as self-consciousness. Feelings of unease arise, and fantasies begin to take the form of a threatening, self-assured and confident rival.

What we see in an infatuation is the activation of parts of ourselves that would be conscious had we not learned to repress them through personal and/or collective experiences. The activation that occurs with the projection of the anima or animus opens the floodgates to the unconscious and releases its contents into consciousness.

IN DREAMS WE SEE OURSELVES

Like other aspects of the unconscious, the anima and animus sometimes make themselves known in dreams. We can see, in the dream series presented in Chapter V, the animus of the dreamer, "Harriet," expressing itself through the images and "plots" of her dreams. Because the animus is fed by, in her case, the archetype of the masculine, a graphic conception of this archetype is presented in Figure Two. Note that for every male in her life there is both a positive and negative image. Not all the images are of equal weight. In Harriet's case, the most influential male in the formation of her animus was her father, and especially the negative image of her father. He and the man with whom she was infatuated at the time the dreams took place dominated the series.

Dreams are not haphazard occurrences. They tell us something about ourselves, comment on our relationships, the state of our psyches and our yearnings, and they reveal the responses of our unconscious to important events. Sometimes dreams seem to carry messages from the

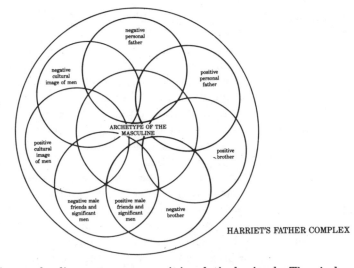

negative
personal
father

negative
cultural
image of men

positive
personal
father

ARCHETYPE OF THE
MASCULINE

positive
cultural
image
of men

positive
brother

negative male
friends and
significant
men

positive male
friends and
significant
men

negative
brother

HARRIET'S FATHER COMPLEX

As confusing as the diagram may seem, it is relatively simple, The circles overlap because the contents of the complex are merged in the unconscious. The core of the complex is the archetype of the masculine: in women, the animus.

Fig. 2   Archetype of Masculine

unconscious and to repeat the messages until the dreamer consciously grasps their import. Although some people insist that they dream only occasionally, what they should say is that they remember few of their dreams; those in all likelihood are "important" dreams, that is, dreams that probably contain some kind of message which, unfortunately, can only be glimpsed in part. Because the interpretation of dreams is an accepted analytic tool, analysands are always instructed to record their dreams upon awakening, the time when one's dreams are most vivid.

Most dreams during emotion-laden periods of one's life, such as infatuation or analysis, are clearly related to each other and can be seen to form a series. The unconscious seems to tell the dreamer through images the meaning of what he or she is experiencing psychically. In the series of eight dreams that are presented in Chapter V, it is possible to trace the psychical development of an infatuation from the initial projection of the dreamer's animus to the point where she begins to regain her equilibrium.

The dreams occurred over a period of about three months, the first on the night after my analysand met her new lover, and the last while the relationship was changing. The last dream is unusual in that it signals the end of the infatuation, something that rarely is so explicit in a dream. The woman experienced many dreams during the infatuation other than those reported here, but they either repeated contents that had already been interpreted or were related to other aspects of her life.

I am often asked during lectures how people tend to respond to interpretations during an infatuation. A person in love while in analysis is no more or less receptive to dreams and to understanding them than is any other dreamer. I know from experience, however, that it is difficult to persuade an infatuated analysand that her or his dreams relate to more than just the projection of the anima or animus because that is all the analysand is interested in hearing about at that stage. The unwanted interpretations of dream images fall into the same category as unsolicited advice from a parent or friend—in one ear and out the other. One's blindness to a lover's faults when one is infatuated makes one deaf to warnings of possible danger. When an affair ends, and especially if it has ended disastrously, it is extremely important to understand, at least after the fact, what was going on during the infatuation in order to make sense of how and why the affair ended as it did. The post-affair analytical work can be an important experience for the future and may be a valuable contribution to individuation. If I were to tell an analysand during an infatuation that separation and acrimony would be the logical outcome of his or her affair, I would be conjuring even if I could support my prediction with incontrovertible psychological evidence. Such evidence becomes available only with time.

The beginning of the end of the infatuation described through the dreams in Chapter V occurs at the dreamer's "magic moment." The "magic moment" occurred in this infatuation when, for the first time, a power struggle arose between the lovers and a compromise was reached on a conscious level. The subject of the compromise is irrelevant; what is significant is that the compromise meant the loss of something important to the dreamer because she was afraid to risk the loss of closeness. Nevertheless, according to her perception, her lover had won and she had lost. That was the moment when the infatuation took a sudden turn.

Because each love affair is unique, there are no universal signposts signaling the approach of important choices along the way, and no generalities to be made. Much of what goes on in an infatuation is unknowable at the time; hence working through dreams retrospectively provides the objective view that is needed to understand what happened and why during the period of great passion.

NOTES

1. Abridged edition. New York: Harper & Row, 1979. (Unabridged edition published in 1977).

2. Stone, *op. cit.* p. 339. (Conclusion to Chapter 10, "Upper-Class Attitudes and Behaviors").

CHAPTER V

DREAMS

Dreams are composed of figurative rather than concrete images. The unconscious can comment on one's psychic experiences only within the confines of what we might call its vocabulary; thus the language—images—of dreams must be interpreted to be understood. The interpretations are presented here at two levels: the first consists of the basic interpretations which are directly related to the dream images and the "story" of the dream. Readers with little experience in Jungian dream analysis will find these interpretations easy to grasp. The second-level interpretations are comprehensive and should be read after those at the first-level; they are directed to my professional colleagues and students of Jungian thought and are based on concepts that may not be appreciated by all readers. Hence they are presented in the end notes. However, readers who are curious about the subtleties of comprehensive interpretations will find the latter an interesting and rich experience.

The Dreamer

Harriet, the analysand whose dreams are presented here, was in her early thirties when I first saw her. She was attractive, quite successful in her profession, and had had several previous affairs. She was the fourth child in an agricultural family. She had one brother and two sisters. From an early age, her relationship with her mother had been strained, and in

81

order to feel safe, she developed an intense relationship with her father. He abused her trust, however, by sexually seducing her when she was fourteen. The experience left her with a strong sense of abandonment as well as other reactions. From then on, understandably, her feelings for her father were ambivalent, especially when she recalled their early closeness against the fact of the subsequent seduction.[1]

I first saw Harriet several months after her last relationship, which had been broken off by her partner. Like her earlier affairs, it had begun and disintegrated rather predictably, leaving her feeling abandoned and misused. Her reaction during the first year or so in analysis was to gradually sink into a state of stagnation in which she felt lonely, isolated, more dissatisfied with her job than ever before, and disconnected from her friends. She intentionally foreswore all relationships with men during that period. The resolve vanished when she met Hans, however. When a friend introduced them to each other, Harriet felt an immediate attraction to him.

Harriet's infatuation with Hans manifested itself in the many ways described in Chapter II. The lovers experienced all the effects of the projection of the anima/animus and of the lowering of consciousness. The need to bring each other into their past lives led to the sharing of confidences: anecdotes about growing up, family relationships, triumphs, and old faux pas.

At this point the question arises whether Harriet told Hans that she had been victimized by her father. The answer is no, and for two reasons. Not only were these reasons important to Harriet in particular, but also they are important to all individuals experiencing certain kinds of childhood traumas. I should note at this point that Harriet had been in analysis for some period before she even revealed the incest experience to me.

One reason Harriet did not confide the experience to Hans was her predictable feeling of shame. Analysts meet over and over in their practices a shameful response from clients who have been sexually abused. Like young children and victims of rape, the victims of abuse egocentrically blame themselves for its occurrence. The response of self-accusation is, of course, reinforced by our culture, which often blames victims for having been wounded. Thus it would have been impossible early in the relationship for Harriet to risk exposing her shame to Hans. In fact, I was the only one she had ever told about it.

The second and more disturbing reason for not revealing the incest is, paradoxically, that Harriet told herself it was not a "big deal." She told herself that her shame was exaggerated and that the experience was of no particular importance in her life: she was well-educated, held a responsible position in the community, had many good friendships, and liked adventure. In order to minimize her feeling of shame, she had identified with her father's self-serving argument that the incest had no significant impact on her and was of no importance in her development. (This same attitude was expressed by a police officer when one of my clients reported that she had been raped at knifepoint. He said, "You look no worse for the wear.")

Harriet suffered the dual and paradoxical burden of feeling (erroneously) shame for having "caused" the incest, and at the same time not being able to experience "in her bones" how much the incest had hurt. These conflicting experiences of the incest kept her silent. She thought that if she told Hans, he might say that she was to blame or that the experience was not important or significant, and consequently that he would not empathize with her. Such a prospect was potentially too painful to risk. We can therefore conclude that even during infatuation we relate only those incidents from our past which, although perhaps still painful, are not fraught with the kind of conflict that incest left in Harriet's life. Nevertheless, the conflict was played out through Harriet's animus, as we shall see in some of her dreams.

Harriet had the first of the dreams making up the following series the night after she met and was attracted to Hans.

The Dreams

DREAM ONE

Beautiful weather. Near the Mediterranean Sea. Many young people are around. They are building a house out of stone. It will be very beautiful. I go over to them and look around. I would like a house like this one. While I am looking around, and over a wall, I see a pile of dreck* in the distance and feel very sad to see this. Then I am sitting with the Queen of England and Lady Diana at a table, eating with many men. Although the atmosphere is stiff, we are having a good time together.

Associations and Interpretation

The dream has four component parts which must be understood in order to integrate its meaning: regression, heroism, prevailing spirit, and individuation.

*Human excrement that is particularly offensive

The opening images of the dream underscore the feeling tone—
idyllic and animating—of Harriet's first encounter with Hans the night
before. The young people in the dream represent the *regression* of the
budding infatuation: once again, for the umpteenth time, Harriet is
experiencing the activation of her feeling and fantasy life. It is as if she
were again joining the ranks of adolescents who innocently experience
the power of love for the first time. This animating feeling is characteristic of the beginning of an infatuation: we feel younger, more spontaneous, more open to the world of senses and feelings. The account in
Chapter II of what it feels like to be infatuated focuses exclusively on
the concrete experience of the regression from stagnant consciousness
into the earlier, less adapted state of adolescence.

During her pre-infatuatory state of stagnation, Harriet had been
feeling rather pleased because she thought she had successfully created
a conflict-free environment for herself. Only much later did she realize
that the dull pre-infatuation period had been a necessary but also temporary respite. It took the infatuation to propel her back into the world
and to give her the energy of adolescence with which to resume confronting the conflicts generated by her family relationships. The house
under construction in the dream is therefore the potential of a new Self.
This Self under construction is in fact the process of making conscious
what had been up to now unconscious aspects of the Self (the totality
of her personality). We may also call this process "putting the ego in
service of the Self" as opposed to "the ego in service of the outer
world." If Harriet can make conscious and integrate what is activated
in the infatuation, she literally will be living in a new psychic home.
Consciousness of Self is the task of *individuation*.

Harriet had made a number of necessary adaptations to her family
while she was living at home, but the adaptations became unnecessary
after she left. Nevertheless, adaptations, once made, become second
nature and unconscious parts of our persona. They are difficult to throw
off because they start out as protective devices. In Harriet's case, the
early adaptations shielded her from the psychological and physical
intrusions and invasions of other family members.

The house under construction (in the dream) is the possibility of a
new psychological home, one that is generated by the adolescent spirit
which Harriet can feel but not yet understand. Functionally speaking,
the infatuation offers her the possibility of becoming conscious of the
adaptations that are no longer required, thus releasing the energy and
vitality necessary to provide a new perspective on herself, her relationships, and her life.

We may note here that mental health professionals generally recognize adolescence as the stage during which we rebel against parental rules, roles, and expectations, and begin to explore new ways of being in the world. Thus the adolescents in the dream represent Harriet's regression to an earlier state in which she can take up again the uncompleted task of separating herself from her parents.

Parental injunctions, for all of us as well as Harriet, become personality traits, and we unconsciously identify with them and live them out. Infatuation provides us with the energy and desire to recognize, through the lowering of consciousness, other of our personality traits that had been relegated to the unconscious and not lived out because we identified with the parental and cultural ideals that made up the *prevailing spirit* in our and Harriet's life.

The Self makes itself conscious in and through infatuation by allowing the eruption into consciousness of those contents necessary to balance the one-sidedness of the pre-existing prevailing spirit. We can call this process the "Self-under-construction." In Harriet's dream, the prevailing spirit in her life is represented by the Queen of England who, like the queen in fairy tales, symbolizes the prevailing image of woman. The Queen exemplifies the parental and cultural injunctions and ideals which Harriet has accepted: "old-fashioned" (in Harriet's words) virtues such as humility, kindness, imperturbability, generosity, gracious sacrifice, etc. Thus the Queen embodies the prevailing spirit that has ruled Harriet's psychic realm since she was a little girl.

Lady Diana represents the *heroism* or *heroic consciousness* that may some day rule in place of the Queen. We should recall the fairy tale motif mentioned in Chapter IV, in which the old ruler ages and becomes rigid, and the masses produce a hero who overcomes major obstacles, marries the old king's daughter, and becomes a king himself, for Harriet's first dream is typical of this motif. Lady Diana represents the possibility of a new attitude, heroic by nature, that can meet conflicts head-on, overcome them, and become the dominant ruler of consciousness in the end. Concretely, Lady Diana represents the courageous and inquisitive attitude Harriet has consciously developed and which will enable her to meet and overcome the unconscious identification with the old prevailing spirit. At the time of the dream, Harriet would not know that this interpretation related specifically to her old relationship with her parents.

In the world of the unconscious, the prevailing spirit opposes and conflicts with the vital forces of the emerging heroic consciousness. The stiff atmosphere of the dinner party in the dream reflects this opposition.

Harriet easily made the connection during our session between the dream and Hans, the man she had met the night before. She focused, in the session, on the excrement on the other side of the wall that loomed like a threat on the horizon. She associated the excrement with her past love experiences; like the dream, they had started out promisingly and later they had become painful and ugly. The pile of excrement consequently frightened her because she thought she would have to suffer again the pain of love turned, as she said, "to dreck."

Harriet was only too correct in her appraisal of the meaning of the pile of excrement. She would have to confront it again. However, according to the dream, when she did so she would have Lady Diana— the new conscious perspective—at her side; and this ally might enable her to come through the "dreck" with a different outcome.[3]

DREAM TWO

Dream Two occurred about a week after Harriet met and fell in love with Hans, while the two were becoming better acquainted.

> I am in a meadow and can see on a hilltop a beautiful castle. There are a number of children, mostly girls, playing games while they run around naked.

Associations and Interpretation

This dream illustrates the central point of the infatuation. The children represent the childlike playfulness and animation that have been activated in Harriet. We saw in Chapter II that the whole world seems fresh and exciting during an infatuation: we look at things in new and different ways, and we seem to experience once again the flow of life and the spontaneity and curiosity of children at innocent play. Indeed, the regression of an infatuation is the rekindling of the spirited and spiritual child in each of us which has been lost in the maturation and adaptation processes of childhood, adolescence, and early adulthood. The shadow traits that are activated in the infatuation and the activity, spontaneity, openness, and curiosity we experience all stem from the animating effect of the activation of the spiritual child.

The children represent our spiritual child's multiple child-like facets. In Chapter III, I noted that in early life the adaptations we make as a consequence of the reactions we received from our parents and the world result in the repression of parts of our child-like nature that would otherwise be lived out. Each child in Harriet's dream represents a part of her childhood personality which she might live out were it not repressed. It is these parts of ourselves that are activated in the infatuation; they run loose during the early days of falling in love and make us playful.

The setting in which the children are playing—outside the walls of the castle—is significant for its dual nature. On the one hand, the castle and its walls represent the prevailing spirit and its boundaries. We can say, then, that child's play, in relation to Harriet's prevailing spirit, is out of bounds. On the other hand, the castle may represent the "heavenly Jerusalem," a symbol of the Self from which spiritual children emanate and to which they return, which implies that they are extremely valuable contents. The two interpretations are not irreconcilable if we keep in mind that there are always two perspectives from which to view any psychological content, that of the ego and that of the Self. From the first perspective, the child's play is infantile; from the second, the child's play releases the animating energy that is bottled up by the repressive perspective of the ego.[4]

DREAM THREE

I am spending the night in an unknown house. Hans and I are sleeping together. I feel very safe. Then we are under water.

Associations and Interpretation

The dream addresses three distinct aspects of infatuation: the *integration into the Self*, the lowering of the level of consciousness, and *trust*. The house in this dream is identical, symbolically, to the one in Dream One. It is a symbol of the Self that has been activated by the unconscious and then projected during the infatuation onto the relationship. The sleep represents the unconscious aspect of the unfolding drama. When we are asleep we are unconscious of the things going on in and around us, just as we are in an infatuation when, in a sense, we are asleep or unconscious of the true and deeper meaning of the affects and experiences happening to us. All this affect and these experiences belong to and are *expressions* of the Self in its attempts to make itself known to the one-sided ego consciousness; yet the *meaning* of the heightened experiences, feelings, and senses remain unconscious for the time being.

The dream indicates that Harriet is unconsciously identified and infatuated with Hans; that is, her Self has been activated and she is both contained within and overwhelmed by contents of the Self. The ego has lost its capacity to act normally, so the contents of the Self and the affect and attitudes expressed during the infatuation are experienced in a way that was not possible before the infatuation. The ego's loss of power, psychologically, is the result of the lowering of the level of consciousness, that is, unconscious contents (the affects and attitudes of the infatuation) replace the old ego standpoint.

The safety that Harriet feels in the dream expresses the almost instantaneous trust we experience when we become infatuated and are led to reveal so much of what we are: at the same time, the feeling of safety leads to the presumption, often misguided, that the beloved is deeply trustworthy. As we go along we shall see that the matter of safety and trust revolves to a great extent around confusion of the beloved with the contrasexual parent. At this juncture, it is sufficient to point out that Harriet felt great trust in Hans, a trust that was not generated by a history of shared experiences.

The dream also discloses that infatuation occurs on two levels. When Harriet and Hans are in the unknown house they are relating on one level, and when they are in the water they are relating on a different level.

In Chapter IV it was mentioned that each infatuation has both a conscious and unconscious level. When we are aware of all the identifiable attributes that we like and value in the beloved, we are dealing with the conscious aspect. The infatuation, however, does not derive any heat or passion from this level. When Harriet and Hans are in the house, they are on the conscious level and they are asleep to the deeper meaning of the infatuation. The deeper meaning occurs at the unconscious level (represented by the water) where the activation and projection of Harriet's animus and Hans's anima occur (inasmuch as Hans was not my client, I cannot know with certainty whether he truly was infatuated with Harriet).

The conscious aspect of the infatuation is the attraction to those traits in the beloved that have been valued in one's life, family and culture. For a woman, this aspect is likely to result in her being attracted to a man like her father, if he was a positive figure, or one opposite her father, if he was a particularly negative figure. The reverse is true for a man. In any event, the conscious aspect of the infatuation is a union of sorts of the woman's father and the man's mother, of their prevailing spirits. The Queen of England in Dream One expresses this prevailing spirit in Harriet.

The union between the woman's animus and the man's anima—their essential spirits—takes place at the unconscious level of the infatuation. Lady Diana, in Dream One, expresses this fact. She represents to Harriet the heroic new possibilities open to her as well as an anima image for Hans. The tension between the Queen and Lady Diana in Dream One mimics the tension within the lovers; they feel the ecstasy of the emotion of love, yet at the same time they fear the loss of the lover or of separation.

So far then, Harriet's dreams reveal that the infatuation occurred as a consequence of collective (cultural) or parental conditioning, opposed and complemented by a more deeply personal but entirely unconscious process of the projected animus. The collective aspect of the infatuation reflects a continuing and unavoidable identification with the parents and culture. Given that we all live in the modern world, our conscious ideals tend to be more or less similar. Thus when the ego identifies to a great extent with collective or parental ideals, it opposes the instincts and other unconscious contents and seeks to control them. For example, aggression, by almost any Western standard, has little value, and attitudes toward sexuality run the gamut of cultural and sub-cultural ideals from Puritanism to "free love." We saw in Chapter IV that the entire movement for "free love" could be viewed as an intellectual revolution against an earlier collective Puritan ideal. In all cases, however, our egos ultimately lead the defense of sexual mores, as we form collective groups to support the ideals and our identification with them. We lose our conscious connection to the instinctive and energetic aspects as a result.

We can say in an infatuation that there are traits in the beloved we like and admire, but these traits add little to the relationship. Whether we are ready to admit it or not, it is the almost uncontrolled sexual and affective experiences that provide the energy for the relationship. (No wonder Puritans considered themselves bewitched when they became infatuated with unsuitable partners!) It is the projected anima and animus that get the whole process going by activating the dormant instinctive and affective strata of the unconscious. These powerful unconscious contents overwhelm the collective prevailing spirit with which the ego had been identified, but they do not extinguish it. On the contrary, the ego identifies with the anima or animus and unconsciously merges this image with the beloved, uniting the image of the contrasexual parent (a part of the prevailing spirit) with the lover upon whom the anima or animus (a part of essential spirit) has been projected.[5]

DREAM FOUR

I am walking along a path with bushes on either side. There is a man in the bushes who is just like my father. His eyes remind me of him, and they are looking deep inside me. I feel no fear, and see that he is playing a game with me, "hide and seek." I begin to play the game with him. Then I am standing in front of the Art Museum. I am thinking about Hans. I now encounter another man. He is a stranger, and introduces himself to me. He is kind and friendly. I feel trust and I would have thought it impossible to feel such trust so quickly. Then he leaves in a taxi to go home. I had completely forgotten to ask him if he would join me for dinner. But I just knew, then, that he would be there anyway, sometime. The relationship was so strong and clear and unequivocal, even though I had not said much.

Associations and Interpretation

The dream initially introduces Harriet's father and then goes on to bring into the picture both Hans (by means of her thoughts) and her animus (in the form of the kind stranger in front of the museum). In the first part of the dream, Harriet is following a path bordered by bushes. The image suggests the potential for psychological growth that an infatuation entails. Harriet's father, however, is hidden in the bushes. The juxtaposition of bushes and father reminds us that growth is generated by confronting some aspect of our lives that is or has been troublesome. When Harriet's unconscious was aroused during the infatuation, the ambivalent relationship with her father was brought to the surface and her ego was faced with the task of integrating the once-unconscious conflict. In practical terms this meant that memories, feelings, and images arose in Harriet which, upon examination, related to many experiences with her father.

I noted in Chapter II that much of the sharing between lovers centers on their histories and experiences. When Harriet was impelled to tell Hans about her life, what she revealed were old memories, feelings and images. One apparent goal of this sharing is the incorporation of the new love into one's world, but another and equally important aim seems to be the re-experiencing and the integration into consciousness of these lost memories in a new and more balanced mode. However, we cannot integrate all activated contents in an infatuation because the aspects of some contents (e.g., the anima or animus) are projected onto the lover. We see the projected content as belonging to the lover, and thus we cannot integrate it at the moment. The situation is demonstrated most clearly in the dream.

From the image in the bushes, it was clear to Harriet that the game in which she and the father-figure are engaged is connected to her father, and also associated in some way with her feelings for Hans.

Harriet recognized consciously that she could not do anything about these feelings at this point in her day-to-day life, however, because so much of her psychic energy was invested in and focused on Hans. On the other hand, she felt the pain and anxiety of wondering whether she would be heartbroken once more if she let herself fall in love again. She asked herself very seriously if her past disappointments in love would be repeated.

The dream of hide-and-seek reminded Harriet of her ambivalent relationship with her father. She also realized that she had played this game with other men in past relationships. Furthermore, in the past she vacillated between acting dependent or aggressive in trying to bind lovers to her. They responded by playing hide-and-seek with her, a game in which she was the seeker and they the sought. Now she was able to recognize the game as an extension of the relationship with her father.

In Harriet's early years, she had escaped from her controlling and oppressive mother in the safety and security provided by her father. She had played a game with him much like hide-and-seek, in which she pursued him. Later, the game became much more dangerous; he was the pursuer and she the pursued. The incest was a literal enactment of capture. She needed, understandably, to repress not only the pain and memory of her father's betrayal of her trust, but also any positive images of him that may have survived the incest.

When Harriet reached maturity, the game became a motif in her love relationships. The unconscious urge to resolve the psychic conflict relating to her father led her to seek men whom she would have to pursue. Although we can trace this game of hide-and-seek directly to the incest, the game itself is commonly played by people who never have been abused, whether emotionally, sexually, or physically.

In the dream, while Harriet is waiting in front of the Art Museum and thinking about Hans, an unknown but very special man makes his appearance. He is, of course, a character like Hippomenes (the Greek mythological character who was given golden fruits to defeat Atalante in a footrace and so win her hand; see Endnote 7). This man too has been given special gifts by the gods to bedazzle Harriet.

Hans, in the dream, begins to carry or become merged with the image of her father when Harriet begins to play the game of hide-and-seek, but then he also merges with the image of the unknown man when Harriet is in front of the museum.

The Art Museum refers to the continuing creative spirit that has been activated in Harriet by love. When she is standing in front of the museum and thinking of Hans, she confronts the beguiling man. He is not Hans; he represents the animus that mediates between consciousness and unconsciousness. The animus and his mediating function is linked to Hans in the same way that her father was, by association and projection. The activation of the animus at this time could help Harriet come to terms with her actual relationship with her father.

The actual state of Harriet's childhood was extremely oppressive. She adapted to the rejection and her parent's expectations (prevailing spirit) by adopting a compliant and withdrawn persona. She presented herself as nice, friendly, kind, and self-sacrificing. She adopted these traits one-sidedly in order to avoid conflicts with her mother and rejection by her father, from whom she sought security. During adolescence, she lost awareness of the fact that she was more than these adaptive traits which she had assumed in order to survive in her family. In other words, she became unconscious of those of her natural traits that might have been acceptable to people outside her family. Subsequently, the latter traits were activated in infatuations through the animus, the animator and mediator of the unconscious.

If we can imagine the anima and animus expressing themselves as feelings of animation that propel us into life (the essential spirit), then we can see repressed traits as new and attractive aspects of our personality opening us to inhibited activities (e.g., "I haven't done this since I was a child.") By directly living out such activities in an infatuation, we recapture parts of ourselves we had lost earlier. For Harriet the result could have been living out a more active, extraverted, spontaneous part of herself. We all do things we have not done for a long time or behaved in ways that are new to us in an infatuation. If we had no father or mother complex, we could maintain the change forever. However, I noted in the interpretations of Harriet's first dream that the Queen does not die. That is, the old one-sided ego perspective does not just dissolve; it is temporarily overwhelmed by the animating infatuation. All the old adaptations remain to create the tension between the Queen and Lady Diana.

To return to the dream, the unknown man in front of the museum symbolizes the animating force of the essential spirit that has been projected onto Hans. ("He makes me feel so alive!" Harriet said.) This unknown man who, we may assume, has powers bestowed by the gods (we tend to see god-like qualities in our lovers), is an exceptional man. He is not merely mortal; rather, the contrary is true. He knows what Harriet is thinking and what she wants, and he incorporates all the qualities we in the West would ascribe to a loving god. When this god-like animus function is projected onto a lover we forget that the latter must be *told* what we think and feel. We assume that the lover is omniscient as well as trustworthy. But, like Harriet, we are terribly surprised and hurt when the lover also manifests idiosyncracies and does not demonstrate extrasensory perceptivity to know what we want and feel without being told directly. Because the anima and animus remain essentially unconscious, we are able to glimpse their properties only through what has been projected onto the lover.

The question is not whether we are conscious enough of ourself to avoid such a projection. The merging of ourself with another through the projected anima or animus occurs because there is always a part of our Self and of the anima or animus in us that remains unconscious. In this way, the personal aspect of the anima or animus (the contrasexual parental complex: mother or father) and the archetypal mediating aspect of the anima/animus are projected onto the lover.[6]

DREAM FIVE

Harriet had the following dream several nights after Dream Four.

Telephone call from Hans. I say I don't have time to see him. He asks if tomorrow would work. I remain silent. Then he says, "You must decide whether you want to see me or not, or whether you want me to come at all!"

Unquestionably, Harriet wanted to see her lover whenever she could. She called him frequently to invite him to her home. While she is consciously playing the game of pursuing, unconsciously she is playing the game of being pursued. There is in the unconscious a replay of the game with her father, with Hans in the role of the father. Father and lover merge in the form of the lover, and an unconscious union develops between Harriet's ego and the father.

The agony and ecstasy of the infatuation is a consequence of the unconscious struggle between the old prevailing spirit—represented by the Queen in Dream One—and the essential spirit represented by Lady Diana. The Queen's discomfort, metaphorically, comes from her disapproval of certain people whom she thinks are her disobedient subjects. The following dream highlights the intensity of the struggle that goes on unconsciously.[7]

DREAM SIX

Guerilla war. Neighborhood similar to that which I grew up in, with mountains. But it is also like a desert. It is total war. Gunfire everywhere.

I am with good people. I have not been hit yet. We are armed with weapons for our defense.

Associations and Interpretation

Harriet associated the desert with Eritrea, where a civil war was then in progress. However, the dream scene also recalls her own neighborhood, which suggests that the conflict is within her, that it is related to some learned behavior of hers that is opposed to another part of her Self. The good people, of course, are symbolic of the cultural support she gets for being well-adapted, and the bad people represent instincts that she rejects and fears. Psychically, the situation is the classic ego/shadow split between good and evil.

The dream reflects the tremendous internal struggle between her spontaneity and her need to adapt and be "appropriate." During infatuation we experience this struggle painfully in those unguarded moments when we say or do something that embarrasses us, and then we rail against our stupidity. An example of the ego/shadow conflict may occur in unguarded moments when the shadow often arises to make us call our beloved by the wrong name or to forget the beloved's name altogether. How harshly we upbraid ourselves for committing such an unpardonable faux pas!

Harriet felt the ego/shadow conflict whenever she became aware of some inner need to ask for something from Hans. She would question herself over and over: "Will he be mad? Am I asking for too much? Do I deserve it?" She would see herself then as a dependent little girl, frightened to reveal what she wanted from him. To her, asking was taking the risk that Hans would think her foolish or silly. So she would say nothing about her need and Hans would be unaware of her struggle and unspoken desire. Thus Harriet sometimes worked herself into a quasi-depression and ruminated about her inadequacies and fears. Then, of course, Hans would notice that something was wrong. When finally she would tell him about her inner conflict, he would respond with warmth and compassion and Harriet would feel the fool for having been "silly," but this time for a different reason.

Our embarrassment at our faux pas is really aggression turned back on us. We begin to see the way in which aggression functions during an infatuation, when we observe our inflexibility at such times. We can imagine with Harriet that the voice of her self-consciousness is in fact the rigid expectations and disapproval left over from her childhood. It would work something like the following. When Harriet was little she was sensitive to the disapproval of her behavior by her parents. When her mother or father would correct her, either explicitly or otherwise, Harriet would have an instinctive self-protective response, namely anger. The repression of her anger contributed to an identification with her parents' perceptions and control of her, and, at the same time, erected a self-conscious and critical perspective. Harriet learned self-control, but also to channel her aggression, albeit unconsciously, back upon herself as critical self-consciousness.

We must be clear, at this juncture, that we are not aggressive at all times in an infatuation. The aggressive feeling arises as a response to some external stimulus, or as a response to the perception of committing some transgression (from the perspective of the critical self-consciousness). Of course, it is also true that we will see aggressive responses among people in love in other circumstances. For example, the man caught in a traffic jam while hurrying to meet his lover becomes much more impatient and angry than at other times.[8]

How easy it is to lose our sense of self-contentment, and then to have a dream like the following:

DREAM SEVEN

Hans and I are together. I am, however, the one who has to do all of the motivating. He is so unwilling, even though I do everything to make him love me. Then, we meet Bea [a woman friend of Harriet's]. While I am cleaning a place for us on the bench, Hans sits next to Bea and kisses her. I see this and go to him, and say, "Well, you're in love with her, aren't you?"

This dream occurred the night after Dream Six.

Inasmuch as Hans had never met Bea, we must assume that she represents a part of Harriet that is consigned to the shadow. In fact, Harriet secretly envies and dislikes Bea because the latter seems so self-confident.

In this dream Hans embodies the function of the animus; he represents that part of Harriet that mediates between the ego (Harriet in the dream) and a shadow part (Bea in the dream). We can see how confusing love is for Harriet and ourselves by trying to sort out what Hans embodies in this dream. First, Hans is the inner animus that is connected to and appreciative of a part of Harriet (her self-confidence), but Harriet is threatened by her self-confidence, because in her view Hans is playing the same game that Harriet's father played with her, namely, I hide and you seek. Thus she thinks she has to do all the motivating, and, in the dream, clean the bench.

Harriet sees Hans as wanting her to chase him and to motivate him to love her because, in part, he actually wants her to "court" him, and in part, she expects such behavior from men. In her relationship with her father, Harriet felt constrained to act a certain way *for him*; thus she does the work, the adapting, and the motivating.

Self-confidence requires an acceptance of ourselves that cannot survive bouts of critical self-consciousness. So Harriet's self-confidence becomes a shadow trait. Hans, the animus in her dream, likes and responds to self-confidence, but as a symbol of her father as well, Hans requires that she sacrifice her self-confidence to pursue and motivate him. We cannot even begin to know what the real Hans wants because of the confusion of roles that are projected onto him: as the father he pulls in one direction, and as the animus he pulls in the other. Thus we can say here that the father pulls her towards regression, whereas the animus impels her to progress and to integrate the part of herself represented by Bea.

The childlike naturalness Harriet felt early in the infatuation began to give way to tension and anxiety as she realized she must do the motivating, that is, keep their relationship alive. Then a simple little incident occurred, seemingly inconsequential, but which marked for her the "magic moment" when she lost control of herself.

One night Harriet had tickets for a concert and she asked Hans to accompany her. He said that he preferred going to F_____, about an hour's drive each way, for dinner at a particular restaurant. Harriet had two options: she could stick to her plan and go to the concert alone or with a friend, or she could give the tickets away and accompany Hans. Unfortunately and predictably, she chose the latter. This was a wholly unnecessary compromise; it was not done out of love or desire, but for fear that Hans would be angry if she did not go with him, and also because of the excessive dependency generated by the projections of her father onto him. Here, of course, we can see how her "motivating" and "cleaning the bench" conflict with her self-assuredness, which is represented by Bea.

At this point, the spirited and spiritual child born of the infatuation became the abandoned child, abandoned because of Harriet's need to adapt to her father. In fact, Harriet had been abandoned by her father when his requirements of her conflicted with her natural development. We are all abandoned to some degree when the imperfections of humanity (our parents and culture) overpower natural development. No parent allows nor can society permit development to take place completely *fear of giving up on = abandonment* *

along the natural gradient; socialization demands limitation. To a child, however, the imposition of limits is felt as rejection and abandonment, no matter how it is expressed.

At the "magic moment" in the infatuation, we compromise something in ourselves needlessly because of our compulsion to conform to the relationship with our parents, and thus we begin a pattern of behavior that resolves the tension between the anima or animus and the contrasexual parental image (Hans as both projected animus and father). Gradually, as the compromises in the relationship become habitual, the beloved takes on more and more aspects of the contrasexual parent's image (Harriet's father) and the spiritual child becomes the abandoned child, untrusting and fearful of loss, while the lover is seen as the parent who demands adaptation—and so the adapting lover abandons herself or himself to the other.

Another example of a "magic moment" comes to my mind. It shows how what at the time seemed to be an apparently minor incident can have far-reaching consequences. My analysand, whom I had been seeing for some time, was a thirty-year-old male. He fell in love with a woman (she later became his wife) who was interested in analysis. Early in their relationship he often told her minor details of what had occurred during our sessions; the details tended to be interesting but not intimate. After one session he felt depressed and distracted, and she asked what had triggered his mood. He said that he did not want to talk about the material. He did not intend to shut her out but he needed privacy to permit the work of our session to incubate. Nevertheless, she cajoled and playfully teased him until, finally, he told her. Now began a pattern in their relationship in which he revealed much of his inner conflicts and she became his mother-confessor. However, he unconsciously developed a belief that was far more destructive, that is, that he *was not entitled* to privacy or a separate world. The woman was by no means to blame for this belief. She was guardian of neither his introversion nor his need to give analytic materials time to incubate. She could not have known the value privacy held for him. Furthermore, it was up to him to protect his inner world. Of course, years later, when he realized that this incident had been his "magic moment," he felt a surge of anger at his wife for "forcing" him to talk.

When the pattern of compromising takes shape and the partner "becomes" a parent, we feel ourself to have been placed in the same inferior position that as children we were to our actual parents. The adapting partner in the infatuation (however, keep in mind that both partners are to some extent adapting) then senses the lover's capacity to reject and abandon; consequently, he or she abandons herself or himself first, rather than be abandoned by the lover. Spontaneity is unconsciously sacrificed along with the abandoned trait (privacy, for example), and the spiritual child becomes the abandoned child, more concerned with holding on to what it has than finding pleasure and fulfillment in the relationship. At that moment we cannot recognize that different interests and desires are essential facets of a relationship, and that conflicts invariably arise out of such differences. We see the differences as negative and requiring more adaptation. The child's natural sense of entitlement to her or his natural (and by no means negative) Self gives way to the feeling of abandonment, and the blame for the changed situation is projected onto the lover-cum-parent.

To put this dream in its proper context, we must recall the tension of the infatuation. In the outer world, Harriet is asking herself, with periodic feelings of panic, what does Hans want from her? What must she do to please him and how can she please herself as well? What must she do to have both ends? Does he want her to pursue him? Does he want her to be coy? Is she asserting her needs when and if she pursues him or is she being aggressive and intrusive?[9]

DREAM EIGHT

> Hans has a girlfriend who is two months away from giving birth to his child. She is a refugee. A very simple person, uncomplicated. Finally, Hans talks to me. I say almost nothing. He says he is sorry he has hurt me. I let him know he has "shit" on me.

The refugee[10] is clearly a victim of the war between the ego and the shadow (see Dream Six). She is in flight from, on one hand, the rigid ego attitude that represses spontaneity, and on the other hand, the seemingly negative (but actually frightening) contents of the shadow (e.g., self-assuredness) that have been activated in Harriet. A mother-to-be, the refugee represents Harriet's potential to develop the new perspective about herself which has been brought to the surface by the inner conflict. Let us examine the image of the pregnant woman closely and concretely to understand the psyche's possibility and the delicacy of the work.

Harriet's parents were unable to nurture her in the way she needed for her personality to develop along its natural gradient. Thus she internalized a method of *self-mothering* that was, for all intents and purposes, stern, rigid, and rejecting. She could not *feel* her value or the value of the different facets of her personality. When she became infatuated with Hans, however, she began to feel the animation of those facets (expressed in the dream by Hans as both father and lover). Hans personifies, in this dream, a connection to an image of a new mother and to a new life formed of the union.

The flight that made the new mother a victim of the war between repression and spontaneity is unfortunate but necessary. Harriet cannot, at this time, recognize and integrate the image of her father projected onto Hans; all she sees is that Hans wants things from her, and that she must be accommodating if she is to hold on to his love. She cannot see that the animating feelings of the infatuation offer her the possibility of a new kind of self-mothering.

We should not blame Harriet for seeking security. We all want security, but we each define it according to our individual experiences; in Harriet's case, security comes when she adapts and accommodates. The potentially nurturing mother of this dream, who could support her true nature, is put to flight by the raging internal conflict between her ego and shadow; thus the net result is the end of the infatuation and the onset of a new stage in the relationship.

In Harriet's first dream about her infatuation with Hans, a pile of dreck lay in the distance. In this last dream, she accuses Hans of having dumped the dreck on her. This projection arises out of her deeply felt pain in pursuing, motivating, cleaning, and accommodating her father/ Hans, which brought her to the next stage in the relationship, a stage that I call equilibrium but is, in fact, more accurately termed a pseudo-equilibrium.

NOTES

1. Although wounded by the incestuous experience, Harriet was able to complete her secondary education, go through professional training, and embark upon a professional career. The primary area of her disturbance, of course, was in her relationships with men. For all practical purposes, nevertheless, the fact of the incest is irrelevant to this demonstration of how the process of infatuation is revealed in dreams. I do not mean that the incest was unimportant in the analysis, but that it did not prevent her from falling in love in the same way that other people do. Harriet had no *pathological* residue as a result of her incestuous experience.

Without minimizing the incest, let me say that we all have had experiences and have memories that shape our complexes. All of us have had to cope with one or another kind of trauma in childhood. These traumatic experiences may have shaped our personalities but they have little effect on the psychological *processes* of our development.

Thus let us accept the fact that Harriet behaved in certain ways and had certain feelings identifiably related and consequential to the incest, and that the experience also influenced her choice of the type of man with whom she fell in love.

2. *Dream One*. The house under construction signals a new beginning in the individuation process. In the dream, the house is circular and the walls are made of stone. The construction of the building is an archetypal image of the creation of the Self by the Self; that is, the Self in its unconscious and unformed state begins to make itself known in an infatuation, and it is symbolized by the house and circular wall. The latter is a mandala symbol of the boundary or *temenos* of the Self, and represents the limits or edge between the outer and inner worlds. In an infatuation this boundary is, of course, experienced as the withdrawal of energy from our everyday responsibilities and the concentration of the energy onto the image of the beloved and our own subjective experiences of the infatuation.

The alchemists imagined that base metals could be transformed into gold through a series of operations. The initial *coniunctio* is an unconscious union of masculine and

100

PHILOSOPHORVM.

Nota bene: In arte noſtri magiſterij nihil eſt ſecretum
celatū à Philoſophis excepto ſecreto artis, quod artis
non licet cuiquam reuelare, quod ſi fieret ille ma
lediceretur, & indignationem domini incurreret, & apoplexia moreretur. ⚹Quare omnis error in arte exiſtit, ex eo, quod debitam

C ij

I

feminine, or spirit and soul, at the beginning of the alchemical process. This was
represented in the *Rosarium Philosophorum* (C.G. Jung, *The Psychology of Transference, CW* 16, p. 213) as the left-handed union of the king and queen (Picture One).

In *The Psychology of the Transference* (*CW* 16), Jung interprets this drawing as
follows:

> We must stress above all else that it depicts a human encounter where love plays a decisive
> part. The conventional dress of the pair suggests an equally conventional attitude in both
> of them. Convention still separates them and hides their natural reality, but the crucial
> contact of the left hand points to something "sinister," illegitimate, morganatic, emotional,
> and instinctive, i.e., the fatal touch of incest and its "perverse" fascination. (*CW* 16, p.
> 212)

The Queen in Dream One represents the conventional, collective attitude of the dreamer. It will become apparent later that the collective attitude plays an exceedingly important role in the equilibrium of relationships. The theme of incest also arises during the equilibrium, as the partners symbolically become children of the same psychic "parents." The dreck that is kept at a distance provides a stark contrast to the general tone of the dream. Later it will become apparent that the alchemical stage of the *nigredo* (also known as the *mortificatio*) is intimately connected to the original *coniunctio*. The *nigredo* of the alchemical process is the blackening of the image of the beloved, which begins to take place when the infatuation abates.

3. *Dream Two*. Jung says that the conventional dress hides the lovers from their true natures. In this dream Harriet sees the naked children, and is herself the undressed child in the relationship. The playfulness and spontaneity of the infatuation are the indicia of this childlike nakedness with Hans. We must keep in mind how difficult it is, at other times, to be playful and spontaneous, to be like children, when we are trying to impress and show ourselves off.

The alchemist's work was to reduce the metal or stone to its rudimentary state, to undress it, and then to operate on it to transform it from its contaminated state into gold. We must recall all manners of contamination which occur in our everyday life, when we feel we must not only contain, but repress parts of ourself, in order to feel acceptable. Thus we put on conventional dress and look alike, sacrificing our individuality, even losing sight of it. The nakedness returns us to an earlier, childlike state of being, to a time before we were so contaminated, from which we may again grow along a more natural gradient. However, the first dream reminds us that the conventional dress remains in our closet, and is not extinguished by the animation of the infatuation.

5. *Dream Three*. An unconscious identification between the lovers takes place in which the two become one. Pictures Two and Three show the naked king and queen immersed in the water, an image which dramatically parallels Harriet's third dream. Jung's commentary illuminates the pictures and the process.

> The real meaning, therefore, is Goethe's "higher copulation," a union in unconscious identity, which could be compared with the primitive, initial state of chaos, the *massa confusa*, or rather with the state of *participation mystique* where heterogeneous factors merge in an unconscious relationship. The *coniunctio* differs from this not as a mechanism but because it is by nature never an initial state: it is always the product of a process or the goal of endeavour. (*CW* 16, p. 252)

The initial *coniunctio* is, however, imperfect because it is unconscious and because a part of the united content consists of collective ideals. There is, in this third dream, as in the drawing, an upper and lower *coniunctio* that represent a collective conscious union and an anima and animus union, respectively. The two levels of the unconscious psyche are activated and united in the same way that the lovers are united. The upper *coniunctio* consists of all the qualities that the lovers know they like about one another, and which are acceptable within their respective community ideals. There is no energy or passion associated with this *coniunctio* because there is no tension in this aspect of the relationship. It is, on this level, as though one were having tea with one's sister or brother. The lower *coniunctio* carries all the passion and animation because it is stripped of adaptation and convention, containing as it does the instinctive and spiritual aspects of the unconscious psyche.

The tension between the Queen and Lady Diana (Dream One) mimics the tension within the lover who feels the ecstasy of the emotion of love and, at the same time,

ROSARIVM

corrũpitur, necp ex imperfecto penitus fecundũ
artem aliquid fieri poteft. Ratio eft quia ars prí
mas difpofitiones inducere non poteft, fed lapis
nofter eft res media inter perfecta & imperfecta
corpora, & quod natura ipfa incepit hoc per ar
tem ad perfectionẽ deducitur. Si in ipfo Mercu
rio operari inceperis vbi natura reliquit imper
fectum, inuenies in eo perfectionẽ et gaudebis.

Perfectum non alteratur, fed corrumpitur.
Sed imperfectum bene alteratur, ergo corrup
tio vnius eft generatio alterius.

Speculum

II

fears the loss of the loved one and separation. Edinger, in his article on the *coniunctio*,
calls this stage "the lesser *coniunctio*." He writes,

> The lesser *coniunctio* occurs whenever the ego identifies with the contents emerging from
> the unconscious. This happens almost regularly in the course of the analytical process.
> The ego is successively exposed to identifications with the shadow, anima/animus and the
> Self. Such contaminated *coniunctios* must be followed by *mortificatio* and further *separa-
> tio*. A similar sequence occurs in the extraverted aspect of the process. The ego identifies
> with certain groups, individuals, institutions and collectives . . . these identifications are
> contaminated mixtures, containing both an individual's potential for noble loyalties and
> object love, and also unregenerate desires for power and pleasure. (Edinger 1982, pp. 5–
> 24)

CONIVNCTIO SIVE
Cottus.

O Luna durch meyn vmbgeben/vnd suffe mynne/
Wirstu schön/ starck/vnd gewaltig als ich byn·
O Sol/ du bist vber alle liecht su erkennen/
So bedarfstu doch mein als der han der hennen.

ARISLEVS IN VISIONE.

Coniunge ergo filium tuum Gabricum dile=
ctiorem tibi in omnibus filijs tuis cum sua sorore
Beya

III

The collective nature of the initial *coniunctio* reflects the continued identification with the personal aspects of the contrasexual complex. In an infatuation, the upper *coniunctio* is the union of collective ideals or prevailing spirit shared by the couple. The lower *coniunctio*, the truly passionate and yet unconscious union, unites the anima and animus and, with them, activates the instincts connected with them. It is the anima and animus union, together with the activation of dormant instincts, that provides the energy and the fascination of the relationship. These powerful unconscious contents overwhelm the prevailing spirit but do not extinguish it.

6. *Dream Four*. In the first dream, Lady Diana represents the possibility of a new feminine identity for Harriet *if* she can integrate the traits which have been repressed and are now activated in the infatuation. In order to free these traits from their bondage

in the unconscious, she must have a logos, an attitude which knows their value, and the courage to confront the collective world within her and outside—which at the time of her dream she thought would be shocked and disgusted if she deviated from its norms. The *Aurora Consurgens*, an alchemical tract ascribed to Thomas Aquinas, details this problem rather well. The Third Parable is called: *Of the Gate of Brass and Bar of Iron of the Babylonish Captivity*. It starts out:

> He who break in pieces my gates of brass and my bars of iron shall also move my candlestick out of its place, and shall break asunder the chains of the prison of darkness and feed my hungry soul . . . (Von Franz, *Aurora Consurgens*, p. 73)

This plaint comes from the anima of the alchemist, repressed into the world of the unconscious, where she has been chained and held captive. The anima of the alchemist is, structurally, the same character as Lady Diana. The unknown male figure of Dream Four is thus the alchemist, or *logos*, which values that part of the soul or personality repressed and hidden from view by a rigid prevailing spirit. We will see in a moment that the refugee woman represents the same content, a new feminine possibility in conflict with old collective ideals and identity.

Harriet has no chance to be transformed and integrated while she remains identified with her father, her father's image of her and the world, and a collective prevailing spirit which devalues what is true in her. She desperately needs to develop a relationship with this unknown figure who has both the ability and courage to break the chains of her captivity in the unconscious. He also has the objectivity to hold her distant from the game of hide-and-seek she plays with men, and to find a new outlook on the nature of her relationships.

7. *Dream Five*. The game Harriet plays with her lovers recalls the Greek myth in which Atalante is pursued by her suitor Hippomenes. Atalante was the daughter of a Greek king who had desperately wanted his first-born to be a son; instead he was given Atalante. Although there is some disagreement over the reason, she was raised in a forest and became an accomplished archer and runner. Because of her beauty, she attracted suitors by score. They tried to woo her despite the severe conditions she imposed on them. She promised to marry any man who could defeat her in a foot race; but, if he lost, she would kill him with an arrow from her bow. Although she gave her would-be suitors a head start, none was able to outrun her. Finally, Hippomenes came along. He brought with him three golden apples from Dionysos's garland which had been given to him by Aphrodite. When Atalante was shown the apples, which were filled with an irresistible love magic, she "was seized with amorous madness" (K. Kerényi, *The Heroes of the Greeks*, pp. 113–120). During the race, Hippomenes threw the apples at her feet and, when she stopped to pick them up, he raced past her to the goal and defeated her.

As the discarded feminine—or, in our culture, nature relegated to the world of the unconscious (the forest)—Atalante represents the fascination with nature and the instincts that are activated in an infatuation. She is captured and tamed by the patriarchal prevailing spirit that opposes and competes with the instincts. The king, the patriarchal prevailing spirit, values only intellect, rules and order, and rejects the feminine attitude represented by his daughter. Today as then, Eros and feeling (the apples given by Aphrodite) are rejected by our prevailing spirit, which is patriarchal and rigid, and we are at the mercy of the prevailing spirit until our feeling life is activated. In concrete terms, the myth is about the competition between masculine and feminine, between Eros and Logos, and between essential spirit and prevailing spirit that takes place during an infatuation, when the natural and repressed contents of the personality are activated.

Applying the theme of this myth to Harriet may help to clarify its relevance to her.

Seeking safety and comfort with her father, Harriet became the daughter of his and the culture's patriarchal ideals and images. She took on, in concrete ways, values and an identity which he liked and expected. Thus, in many ways, she became a reflection of him but at the cost of repressing her true nature.

The repression relegated her nature (Lady Diana), like Atalante, to the forest of the unconscious. In the infatuation, Hans becomes Hippomenes who, with the magic of love, arouses her passion. He is the animus in Harriet igniting her unconscious feminine or Atalante-like nature that has been repressed as a consequence of her relationship with her parents and culture. We must remind ourselves at this juncture that the infatuation is like a midcourse correction, a consequence of a one-sided conscious perspective that has restricted and narrowed the personality's field of perception and behavior.

From the myth, we can see that the arrival on the scene of the animus in the form of Hippomenes is the consequence of the self-regulating nature of the psyche: it provides balance to a one-sided conscious perspective. In the myth, the one-sidedness is addressed by Aphrodite, the goddess of love, who gives Hippomenes the magic apples; the latter are associated with Eros, Aphrodite's son and the God of Love. The competition between Atalante and Hippomenes is archetypal in nature. Having concluded that the game of pursuit is a competition during an infatuation, the goal is to integrate the feminine and to unite masculine and feminine, nature and spirit, through love. Unfortunately, it is not so easy. The game does not conclude with the loving couple living happily ever after. According to the myth, Artemis turns the lovers into lions who must forever remain chaste. In the world of lovers, the game of pursuer/pursued is an unconscious attempt to capture the beloved and integrate the repressed feeling and animation which has been projected on them through the anima or animus.

The father's hide-and-seek in the fourth dream provides more understanding of the connections between Harriet's father, lover, and animus. The images tell us that Harriet once again is in the grip of the archetypal game of reunifying her masculine and feminine natures. The game gives her the opportunity to come to terms with her repressed feminine nature by confronting her relationship with her father and his patriarchal values.

The fifth dream demonstrates the way that the game of hide-and-seek which Harriet played with her father has been brought into her relationship with Hans. Hans is, unbeknownst to Harriet, being confused with her father, and symbolically she becomes his daughter. This "incestuous" quality of relationships is even more apparent in married couples. In the alchemical *coniunctio* the marriage of the king and queen (pictures one through three) have also to do with the incest theme. Jung writes that:

> At the same time, the intervention of the Holy Ghost reveals the hidden meaning of the incest, whether brother and sister or of mother and son, as a repulsive symbol for the *unio mystica*. (*CW* 14, p. 472)

Inasmuch as the alchemists were men and the image of mother-son incest is specific to masculine psychology, we must turn the parallel around for a woman. In this way we see that the incest for a woman may concern brother-sister or father-daughter. Later, it will become clear that the conflict between the incestuous drive and the drive for individuation within the relationship will be resolved in favor of psychological incest.

In the outer world of a relationship, a lover is unconsciously assimilated into the Self of the partner, and the world outside this union becomes threatening. The isolation of the early part of the relationship serves the psychological purpose of creating a space within which the incestuous *upper coniunctio* and the passionate *lower coniunctio* may take place. We will see later that the *separatio* produces a similar but opposite situation.

Whereas in the initial *coniunctio* a lover represents a form of psychological salvation, in the *separatio* salvation seems to come from the world outside the relationship.

The *upper coniunctio* is represented in this dream by the merging of the father with the lover image. The *lower coniunctio*, on the other hand, is the merging of the lover and animus images. In the *Mysterium Coniunctionis*, Jung explains that

> Since the soul animates the body, just as the soul is animated by the spirit, she tends to favor the body and everything bodily, sensuous and emotional. She lies in the chains of Physis, and she desires "beyond physical necessity." (*CW* 14, p. 472)

Soul, to Jung, is the anima of the man—projected into matter, or the world—who must be freed both from the world and the unconscious if she is to have life and fulfill her function. Jung saw the animus as the spirit of the woman, who essentially is soul herself. In the *Psychology of the Transference* Jung writes that

> Unfortunately, we possess no original treatises that can with any certainty be ascribed to a woman author. Consequently, we do not know what kind of alchemical symbolism a woman's view would have produced. Nevertheless, modern medical practice tells us that the feminine conscious produces a symbolism which, by and large, is compensatory to the masculine. (*CW* 16, p. 302)

If we assume Jung's view to be correct, we would expect to see a different set of images in men than in women. In the last quote but one, Jung says that the soul animates the body, and is animated by the spirit. Soul, we must remember, is relatedness, feeling and Eros. There is, of course, no question that relatedness will animate, or "get the body going," if we recall that the body represents the instincts. In relationships, we are undoubtedly always on the brink of some experience which will satisfy either our sexual, aggressive or relationship instincts. That is, we cannot be relating with someone with our clothes off (symbolically) and not be close to a body experience. We will feel either sexually attracted, or defensive against, or attached to the other individual. Thus the soul animates the body and is in turn animated by the spirit. Spirit is associated, in this sense, with *logos*. If our prevailing spirit is anti-nature, we are cut off from both soul and body. We live, then, in a collectively clothed existence. If, on the other hand, the prevailing spirit embraces what is natural in us, it animates our relatedness (soul), which connects us then to the body.

What we encounter in the dreams of both men and women is, however, a patriarchal *logos*, or attitude which is anti-nature and relegates soul in both sexes to an enchained existence in the unconscious. When soul is enchained in the unconscious, so also is the body. It thus follows that men and women have the same task, namely to struggle against the anti-natural prevailing spirit, or collective consciousness, and to free soul, or relatedness, and body, the instincts, from their enchainment in the unconscious. In this sense only, there is no distinction to make between mens' and womens' psychology.

8. *Dream Six*. This dream foretells the internal struggle between ego and shadow discussed in the main text. Alchemists frequently used the image of war to indicate activity between or among metals that had been exposed to heat. In order to understand the purpose of the war, we must backtrack a bit to the initial *coniunctio*. In the *Aurora Consurgens*, the alchemists begins his treatise with the following:

> All good things come to me together with her, that Wisdom of the south, who preacheth abroad, who uttereth her voice in the streets, crieth out at the head of the multitudes . . .
> (von Franz, *Aurora Consurgens*, p. 33)

In her commentary on the *Aurora*, Marie-Louise von Franz claims that the alchemist's encounter with Wisdom is the symbolic representation of the initial *coniunctio* (p. 157

ff, 218). The alchemist, having had a deep and moving encounter with Wisdom, or the body, closely follows her plight throughout the treatise.

Von Franz asserts that Wisdom is a symbol of the collective unconscious (p. 156 ff), and meeting her is analogous to a "numinous encounter with the anima" (*Ibid.*). This identity is important because we must compare her with the refugee in Harriet's sixth dream and Lady Diana in her first. In my interpretation of the first dream I identified Lady Diana as the symbolic representation of a new possibility of feminine life for Harriet. This is a goal of the analytic work, just as integration of the anima is the alchemist's goal. Dream One signals the possibility of the future. Dream Six signals the present conflict between ego and unconscious. In her commentary, von Franz attributes the sublimity of the description of Wisdom to the apparent fact that the alchemist's anima must have been "devalued in the author's consciousness, and that this devaluation is here compensated by the sublimity of the image" (*Ibid.*). This is also the state of Harriet's psyche—valuable aspects of her feminine nature have been devalued, and the first dream compensates this situation. The sixth dream, on the other hand, depicts her present state of mind—where a conflict is raging, but not yet overtly.

9. *Dream Seven*. This dream signals the beginning of the end of the infatuation, the initial *coniunctio*, and raises the specter of the next stage of the alchemical process, *calcinatio*. As we have seen throughout, the infatuated state is extremely fluid. Faults and transgressions of the beloved are unseen or easily forgiven. Obviously, this comes to an end. The inner struggle between ego and unconscious, the confused mixing of the parent with the lover with the anima/animus erupts for the first time, at the "magic moment" I described in Chapters Four and Five. Attitudes harden gradually, as we begin to see not only difference in the other, but more importantly, our own shadow traits. The hardening is a consequence of the inner struggle between ego and unconscious, and our defense against it. The heat of the inner conflict—as described in Chapter Five, our fear of abandonment and embarassment—finally surfaces in that "magic moment," when we see the other as being capable of hurting us, and we defend ourselves by becoming angry, disapproving or withdrawn.

According to Paracelsus, the *calcinatio* is the first stage in the process of transformation, because the initial *coniunctio* is a natural condition of the alchemist's stone, also called the *prima materia*. Paracelsus described calcination as:

> The first step . . . under which is comprised Reverberation and Cementation. Among these three there is little difference so far as relates to Calcination. Here, therefore, Calcination is the principal step . . . By Calcination all metals, minerals, stones, glasses, and all corporeal objects, become carbon and ashes; and this is done in a naked fire, and exposed to the air. By means of this all tenacious, soft, and fat earth is hardened into stone; but all stones are reduced to lime . . . (pp. 151–2) (*The Hermetic and Alchemical Writings of Paracelsus*)

The result of this conflict and hardening is the flight of the pregnant refugee woman in the following dream.

10. *Dream Eight*. It may be hard to imagine how this refugee woman is the same character as Lady Diana in the first dream, but imagine it we must. She is the "soul" of the dreamer activated by the infatuation some three months earlier, when Harriet first met Hans. Pregnancy, in alchemy, is a common image to describe the "cooking" or "incubating" that the alchemist's stone must undergo. In Picture Four, from the *Splendor Solis*, a vase contains the infant stone. The parable that accompanies it says:

> Firstly, a heat powerful enough to soften and melt these parts of the earth that have become thick, hard and baked, as mentioned by Socrates when he says: that the holes and cracks

IV

of the earth will be opened to receive the influence of Fire and Water. (Trismosin, *Splendor Solis*, p. 34)

Not only is this reminiscent of the *calcinatio* in the passage from Paracelsus cited above; it also represents a complete inversion, namely the softening of what has become hard. The infant and mother in this dream represent the possibility of transformation resulting from the infatuation and projection of Harriet's animus onto Hans. The refugee is put to flight by both the raging inner conflict and the hardening attitudes which begin to reestablish themselves in consciousness as the infatuation and initial *coniunctio* come to an end. The receptivity and fluidity of the infatuation begin to give way to a structured relationship with rules and identifiable qualities. It becomes hardened, and so also do the hearts of the partners.

CHAPTER VI

MARRIAGE AND SEPARATION

Not too long ago a client took time in one of the groups to talk about a problem which had often cropped up in her marriage. She and her husband had been having serious conflicts for a number of years, and they could not seem to break out of the pattern. In this particular session, the woman told a story about an argument they had the previous week. She had wanted to feel some intimacy with her husband, and had asked him to hold her. He walked away for whatever reason, and as we might expect, she became angry. The conflict increased, and after not too long he asked, apparently in earnest but with no apparent context, if she were having an affair. This question, posed by her husband so often before, infuriated the woman, and she refused to answer—thus setting the stage for a week-long argument which was still raging as she came to the group.

We all knew that this woman had one or two affairs in the distant past, but that she was faithful now. Several group members supported her, encouraging her to continue to refuse to answer until her husband told her why he had asked. Others in the group wanted to know why she was so hotly contesting the question. The woman responded that she was sick of being on the defensive in such situations. The other members began to see the power struggle she and her husband were engaged in, and told her so. One astute observer even asked if her refusal to answer the question, and her sensitivity to it, were responses to some unresolved feelings about her earlier affairs. The question penetrated like a dagger. Another client said she could have responded to her husband's question with a sympathetic, "no, why do you ask?" And a third group member told her that her husband sounded like an insecure little boy.

I was interested in the problem and finally asked what the husband's question had to do with *her*. We were gradually told about teen-age promiscuity and other behaviors the woman had never mentioned before. She called herself a "slut," a word she used over and over again; but she began to see, as did the other group members, that her refusal to answer her husband's question arose from her unresolved feelings about her affairs, yes, and also out of deeply painful feelings left over from adolescence. For years she had been on the defensive with her husband in order to repress these memories.

Her sense of powerlessness—as well as her affairs—arose out of conflicts felt much earlier in her life. At that moment, with her husband's question squarely before her, she could not see his infantile insecurity. She could not see that she only needed to answer no. In fact, she could see neither herself nor him in any realistic way at all. She could not differentiate herself from her husband, or what he knew from what she knew. She responded to his question the only way she knew how, with a flood of feelings she could not grasp, let alone comprehend.

How did this woman come to find herself in the painful position of defending her right *not* to reassure her husband? How do people, passionately in love years earlier, become engaged in a struggle neither can win, and which results in a pervasive loneliness and alienation neither can tolerate?

BOUNDARIES

The woman in my group defended herself from the pain of remembering and reliving experiences she hoped would remain forgotten. The defense she used was refusal to answer her husband, projection of the blame onto him, and engaging in a power struggle which deflected attention from her underlying guilt and shame. Had she not defended herself she would have felt the pain of remembering her "sordid" past, but she would also have learned, as she did in the group, that her present behavior had nothing to do with her husband's question. She would have been able to see her husband's question as an expression of his insecurity alone. She would not have been at all a participant in his insecurity, to which she could have responded as she felt, sympatheti-

cally, impatiently, or otherwise. The key is that she would have known
what belonged to her, namely her guilt and shame about her past
behavior, and what belonged to him, namely his insecurity.

As an analyst, I am concerned as much with uncovering old wounds
as I am with the assertion of present boundaries. I want to help my
clients learn to differentiate boundaries from defenses, to learn which
boundaries express the natural limits of their personalities. If they must
rely on externally-imposed boundaries (whether from me or anyone
else) before learning to identify their own, then so be it.

A man who consulted me about his impending marriage was un-
nerved by his friends, who said he was insane for wanting to marry a
woman with a congenital arthritic condition that would only worsen
with time. His friends told him that he could not possibly want to devote
his life to the care and love of a woman who would be, in not too many
years, utterly helpless. After several sessions it became quite clear that
he was in fact willing to make the sacrifices necessary to find satisfaction
in a marriage which would be filled with so much pain. He would also
have to manage her life completely: make sure she took her medication,
did whatever exercises were mandated by her condition, and took the
kinds of safety precautions that would endanger neither herself nor the
general public. In other words, he would have to become almost obsessed with her daily rituals, needs, moods and intentions. Can someone
who willingly enters into a relationship which requires so much sacrifice
be truly conscious of his own boundaries? From my perspective, of
course, the answer is yes. His boundaries obviously differed from what
we might call prevailing wisdom, but boundaries he seemed to have.

THE EQUILIBRIUM

We cannot talk about what happens in marriage without seeing events
in context of boundaries and defenses. In the last two chapters we
saw how infatuation blurs boundaries; that is, love captivates two
individuals, causing the lowering of the level of consciousness, which
precipitates fascination and tension. When we left the enraptured couple
in Chapter V, we could not, perhaps, imagine that they would become,
within a few years, embittered and estranged, seeking any handy outlet
for the expression of their disappointment and resentment. We saw how
the infatuation activated dormant unconscious contents, flooding the
lovers with powerfully pleasant but threatening feelings. For some
psychologically astute people, the flood of emotions reminds them of
what life can be, and they are able to see how their pre-infatuation lives

had been stagnant and unsatisfying. But for most, the flood appears as an autonomous emotional event unrelated to their lives before they fell in love. A man who falls in love does not see the powerful feelings belonging to himself, but rather as extensions of his beloved. He does not see the lack of animation in his life as an expression of his relationship with himself and the world, but as a circumstance to be suffered until he meets the right woman. When he does become infatuated, the pleasure, but also the threatening feelings, become embodied in her. She "causes" him joy and pain simultaneously.   *Why pain*

When a powerful event takes place (such as falling in love), a psychological regression may follow. When we can no longer maintain a perspective on the conflict between the pleasure and pain of the infatuation, we unconsciously look backwards for a behavioral model to make sense out of our present predicament. What we see depends greatly upon who we are and what we have been through. When the magic moment I described earlier takes place, it is most often consciously experienced only as one of the adaptations couples arrive at in order to maintain harmony. Most people remember their parents telling them, during adolescence or on the night before the wedding, that marriage requires give-and-take, compromise, even sacrifice. This is exactly what I mean when I say that we look back to our past history. Harriet, the client I described earlier, looked back to her history the night she chose dinner over the opera. She remembered being told that relationships require compromise. She also remembered seeing her father, over and over again, submit to the apparently stronger will of her mother. So Harriet gave up her tickets to the opera, letting go of her own desire according to her father's example. An apparently innocuous difference between Harriet and Hans generated an inner conflict. The answer which leaped to mind, albeit in a mostly unconscious form, was to adapt to Hans' plans. Harriet's motive for adapting was the memory of her mother rejecting Harriet and her father whenever (as it seemed to Harriet) they dared to differ with her. What led Harriet to choose her particular adaptive method was what had worked in the past—namely, surrender. Her excitement and joy at the prospect of seeing the opera with Hans became disappointment instead, and she repressed the disappointment, all in order to solidify her relationship with Hans, and thus to make herself feel secure.

When the initial euphoria of the infatuation begins to wane, each partner begins to see what differences must be dealt with if the relationship is to continue. How they do or do not confront the differences is greatly dependent on their family, cultural, and educational history. If the advice that marriage requires compromise sounds familiar, it is because that particular prevailing spirit is firmly entrenched in our world view. If it seems obvious that Harriet would be disappointed, but that she would repress her feelings, this too is understandable: the prevailing spirit does not pay much attention to painful emotional reactions. *like it or lump it.*

Looking backwards to our personal history entails reexperiencing the adaptations and repressions of our earlier life; we begin to recreate the world we had before we fell in love. The only difference is that we are now doing so with another person, who is trying to do the same thing. The net effect of this struggle is a gradual loss of vitality in the relationship. The animation so eagerly awaited and experienced during the infatuation gives way to unconscious adaptations and compromises which ensure the perpetuation and comfort of the relationship.

The loss of vitality is a direct consequence of finding no meaningful resolution of the differences between the two lovers. By "resolution" I do not mean the *removal* of differences, but their identification and recognition, with a corresponding change in behavior which results in enhancement of the relationship instead of repression. If this doesn't sound impossible, it should. I cannot imagine anyone being so attentive and so conscious as to always know what one feels, when one feels it, how it relates to oneself and one's partner, and what one needs to do in order to achieve a broader view of one's relationship. I have encountered people who believe, and try to prove, that there are couples who are so aware that they never under any circumstances resort to adaptation and repression in order to resolve conflicts. Perhaps. I hesitate to categorically pronounce that *all* couples contend with the problem of adaptation and repression. I do believe that many look backwards to their own history for guidance and security when they confront their partner's otherness, and that, quite naturally, those who do not never find their way to my consulting rooms. Those who adapt and repress often make their way to me only later, when the equilibrium they have so carefully constructed breaks apart.

Adaptation to the partner's personality often mirrors the adaptations we made to our parents, teachers and other authority figures. We can infer that a power relationship begins to arise as adaptations continue. This power is seen in the apparent need expressed by the unconscious refusal to recognize and deal with differences inherent in the relationship. Harriet adapted to Hans because she felt an unconscious or conscious need to have the affair continue, though practically speaking she did not "need" it; she could, and had, survived without it. Her need created the power-relationship, because Harriet began to behave as a child in relation to a potentially abandoning parent. Hans had power, and Harriet had to adapt. Like so many of us, she did not see that her

These adaptations may be predictable and could be "mapped out" + dealt w/ early + taken into acct.

unhappiness, before she fell in love, was an expression of her relationship with *her* world above all. Power enters a relationship when the
partners begin to look backwards, consciously and unconsciously, to
parental models, those attitudes and behaviors which are meant to help
preserve the relationship.

There can be no safety and peace, however, if the partner continues
to perceive and behave in ways that remind us of our differences, and
so of our insecurity as well. Yet while we are adapting to the will and
desires of the partner, we are giving up the animating possibilities of
the infatuation. The woman who loves to dance gives it up for her
partner with two left feet, who self-consciously refuses to make himself
feel vulnerable in order to please his beloved. But it could be just the
reverse; he could continue to take her dancing, each time feeling
more embarrassed and unsatisfied. There is no winning when one's
differences are given up without struggle. We know that this couple
could carry on a years-long fight over dancing, and get nowhere, except
to feel deep resentment and bitterness.

The easiest way for any such conflict to be defused, of course, is for
it to remain unconscious. This is exactly what seems to happen most
frequently during the equilibrium. Each partner represses in himself
much of what seems different from the other, and in turn tries to
suppress in the partner what is different from him. Complications begin
to surface. The dancing woman, resenting the loss of a favorite activity,
becomes critical of some other associated idea. Whether overtly or
covertly communicated, she lets him know, for example, that she does
not like the way he dresses. He feels the criticism, and becomes self-
conscious; he also feels controlled. He sees her as an overly-involved
mother who sticks her nose into his business. If they continue to dance,
and he represses his self-consciousness, he will become critical of
some other and associated idea. She talks too much. Her extraversion
embarrasses him in front of his friends. Whatever it is, she feels picked
on, criticized, controlled. He is a rejecting and demanding father never
satisfied with her as she is.

She does not tell him what she thinks about him, nor he her—at least
not during the equilibrium, when there is enough good will and memory
of the infatuation to stave off the intense need to put the other straight
about just how badly she (or he) is behaving.

In the equilibrium, if one is finally achieved, the couple seems to
work together and resolve conflicts in a well-adapted, even healthy
manner. All tough conflicts, the ones not easily adapted away, are
repressed out of consciousness, to surface again later, when we think

we are beginning to grow tired of our partner, or when she (or he) begins to change for the worse.

THE PSEUDO-EQUILIBRIUM

As far as I can tell, all marriage counseling seems to strive towards the resolution of underlying conflicts and the easily recognizable resentment in unsatisfying relationships. This is a worthy goal, and there are a myriad of books available to tell us all how to enrich our marital lives, resolve our conflicts, express our deepest (or highest) Self, experience that elusive orgasm that stretches our body consciousness, or whatever else it is we are looking for. As I said in the Introduction, this is not a how-to book. When someone comes to me for advice or counsel about how to make a relationship better, I throw up my hands. I tell them I haven't the vaguest notion. Day in and day out I see supposedly well-adjusted, highly intelligent people who get themselves into the mess of their lives with their spouse or lover. This is just as true for marriage counselors as it is for computer operators and truck drivers. The difficulties everyone encounters are an extension of the pattern of resolving the inner and outer conflicts which arise when one first becomes aware that the lover is a very different person.

The equilibrium I described in the preceding section has an external face, one which permits the couple to function together, perhaps even to marry. The dreams we have at this time suggest that the relationship is actually a pseudo-equilibrium, because in the inner world conflicts are apparent and upsetting. I am reproducing below my redrawing of a diagram from Jung's *Psychology of the Transference:*

The direction of the arrows indicates the pull from masculine to feminine and vice versa, and from the unconscious of one person to the conscious of the other, thus denoting a positive transference (love) relationship. The following relationships have therefore to be distinguished, although in certain cases they all can merge into each other, and this naturally leads to the greatest possible confusion:

(A) An uncomplicated personal relationship.
(B) A relationship of a man to his anima and of the woman to her animus.
(C) A relationship of anima to animus and vice versa.
(D) A relationship of the woman's animus to the man (which happens when a woman is identical with her animus), and of the man's anima to the woman (which happens when the man is identical with his anima).

The diagram presents Jung's ideas on the transference relationship, and I am borrowing it to look at love relationships. When two people fall in love, they share a conscious relationship (A) which they can both easily describe: their character traits, habits, likes and dislikes, etc. When they fall in love, however, an unconscious relationship develops as well, the man with his anima (B), which is projected onto the woman (D), the woman with her own animus projected onto the man. Each partner thus perceives the other as extraordinarily animated; the man's anima forms a relationship with the woman's animus (C) and vice-versa.

After the infatuation starts to wane and the work of establishing a down-to-earth relationship begins, the primary union, as it were, is between the partner's respective egos, which, as I mentioned in the last section, look backwards for emotional precedents. The prevailing spirit reasserts itself in order to bring the couple into safer waters. The reassertion of this older prevailing spirit crowds out—represses—the essential spirit which accompanied the projection of the anima (or animus) onto the partner. The affects, images and fantasies which are the expression of essential spirit are also the byproduct of the projection of the anima (or animus). These are also repressed. While the repression serves to stabilize the relationship, it also serves the ego's need to have command of the situation, a control it does not have when we experience unbridled love and insecurity.

The projection onto and identification of a man's anima with his wife, or a woman's animus with her husband, explains the necessity of suppressing those behaviors in our spouse which we cannot tolerate in ourselves. If we need to cool the pitch of our own emotional responses, it does not seem particularly helpful to have our partner maintain his or her own emotional intensity. That situation increases rather than decreases insecurity and tenseness. The repression of our own animation results, then, in a corresponding suppression of the partner's animation. Since this is a mutual activity, both people end up playing a kind of power game, where each controls his own responses, and asks, by word or deed, the other to do likewise.

too bad.

term

ok

yes! a kind of collusion

which explains why outsiders may wonder what the couple sees in each other + ... keeps them together.

We can now look, in close detail, at the activity going on under the surface of a relationship. When we look back to our history to find precedents and behaviors to stabilize the relationship, we identify with images of a collective nature. A man begins to behave in the ways that seem to be acceptable to his father and/or to the culture from which he comes. He becomes, in a sense, the image of Everyman. He also wants his wife to behave as Everywoman who is, of course, his mother, but also the cultural image of woman. The woman is just as anxious to find her own safe niche. She becomes Everywoman for her own purposes, and in turn projects the image of Everyman onto her lover.

When there is some overlap, but not a perfect fit, between the images each lover wishes the other to live out, a number of possibilities arise. They can ignore the differences, those areas in which there is no overlap *1.* between their respective image of who the other ought to be. They can *2,* also pretend the differences are insignificant, or that they have been resolved. And last, they can see the differences as problematical, symptomatic of the larger difficulty, namely, repression and adaptation *3,* away from the animation. Not many people I have encountered over the years choose or even know about this latter alternative. *Too bad, OK,*

I would like to assume that the latter alternative is not chosen, that the couple uses one of the methods, any method, which does not lead to a conscious recognition of the underlying problem. There are no *apparent* problems when the images the partners want for themselves and the other overlap. When differences are ignored, or some pretense is erected to deal with them, the marital relationship remains unclouded as long as its defenses remain effective. To the extent that the couple *i.e. mis-* fight over only *apparent* differences, the conflict is obviously irresolv- *perceived* able. There is no solution to a problem if we are trying to solve the wrong one.

Any conflicts which arise at this point defend those composite ego images and identities. He comes to seem much like his father and her father, she much like her mother and his mother. He looks like he came from her family and she looks like she came from his family. She looks like she came from his world, and he looks like he came from her world. As a matter of fact, they begin to seem like children of the same parents! *E.g. E reminds me of Republican brother at times, + I probably remind her of her father who sold off her horse + had eyes for her girl friend,*

PSYCHOLOGICAL INCEST

Before I get to the heart of this provocative subject, I want to clarify what I mean by a couple becoming symbolically children of the same parents. This is a handy way of identifying the images and roles couples adopt in order to create and maintain a predictable, safe and comforting relationship. Of course, a grown adult is different from his or her real-life parent. By *parent,* I mean the roles and images I have throughout this book associated with prevailing spirit, and which represent the rules of behavior and perception we live by. We all take images from our world to fill in our blank spots, where we do not know what belongs to us, or where we are frightened by what we see in ourselves. And so although we may be relatively free of our personal parents, we all must suffer the consequences of being social animals with a limited capacity for consciousness, self-actualization, and courage. The couple whose bible is *The Feminine Mystique* lives with an image, a parent, just as surely as the young adults whose tender years and lack of experience are seen in their uncritical adoration of their respective parents and their marriages.

The pseudo-equilibrium exists whether a marriage has taken place or not. It is a stage which occurs, regardless of the best efforts of the partners, when one goal of the relationship becomes predictability and security. The effect of the pseudo-equilibrium is the creation of a structure and partnership ethos which permits certain behaviors and excludes others. Metaphorically, the partnership ethos becomes the parent, the partners its children. They may agree to consult one another before making major decisions about their careers, their home, their finances, etc. They may agree that they will have no extra-marital relationships which include sex or romance. They may agree, through a process of negotiation or unilateral fiat, that a number of possibilities of behavior and perception are to be either mandated or proscribed. I remember, for example, one couple who had agreed never to mention the miscarriage the woman had had before their marriage. The agreements people make are wide-ranging, and beyond my limited capacity to cite even a representative sample.

Of greater interest to me are the implicit, unspoken agreements couples come to, which prescribe and proscribe their behaviors, feelings, and perceptions in an equally forceful way. These unspoken rules are the ones most often uncovered only by a marriage therapist. These can be the most subtle to work with, since the control is implicit and easy to deny. In practical terms, psychological incest, like its concrete namesake, can only exist in secrecy. As with actual incest, it rarely is acknowledged openly. The children deny incest because of the shame and humiliation they feel, even though they are unwilling victims. The incestuous parent denies the victimization he or she causes, of course, because of his or her own shame and humiliation, and the obvious terror of being found out. The non-abusing parent denies the incest in order to maintain the familial pseudo-equilibrium, and out of fear of facing the terrible pain of acknowledgement. The other children deny the abuse for fear of implication or that they will be blamed or scape-goated; and, perhaps, fear of betraying someone they mistakenly think deserves their trust.

All of the factors cited above also hold true for psychological incest. The conspiracy of silence, another example of the implicit agreements the couple make, serves the pseudo-equilibrium and the security it creates. Many may think that I am exaggerating the seriousness of the pseudo-equilibrium and psychological incest. On the other hand, anyone who has been divorced will readily recognize how painful and dangerous that complicity is. What starts out as an attempt to create a union which expresses the love we feel for one another in effect becomes the prison men at stag parties are wont to describe. Not only men, however, see the enchainment that marriage can become. Many feminists describe and decry the servitude, even enslavement, of married women. Men's groups, women's groups, political groups of men and women, liberal church leaders, and even popular magazines and journals argue against patriarchal stereotyping and sex role discrimination.

Psychological incest—the repression of what is in us and the suppression of what is in our partner in order to achieve a predictable and secure relationship—creates the roles and expectations which order the partnership. We become the children of these roles and expectations, conforming here, rebelling there, to an authority, our spouse, our lover, who is doing the same thing. All that this relationship was meant to express—the love, the animation, the companionability—gradually becomes, for many if not most, a structure in which we recreate the relationship with our parents, personal or collective. What we have not yet worked out about our individuality becomes the explicit and implicit rules and expectations of the relationship, and which we react to as children, namely by compliance or rebellion, or a combination of both. The husband who does not smoke in his wife's presence out of fear of disapproval in effect creates his wife in the parental images, and out-wardly complies, while secretly grabbing a smoke behind the garage. And when he gets caught, he will vigorously defend his right "to kill himself." All the while, the smoker feels the guilt and shame of being so frightened of the spouse's apparent power and disapproval, but also resents the spouse's apparent caring.

Here is another, equally obvious example of the theme of parental authority, but with a twist. A client was married to a woman who weighed well over four hundred pounds. Her family had a history of heart problems, and she was at great risk of developing cardiac problems herself. My client complained that his wife "ate like a horse." He was concerned about her health, but not once had he ever, in the seventeen years they had been married, said a word about his concern over her weight. Not once. This seemed, of course, a little odd. When I asked him about his failure to express his concern, he told me that they had an unspoken agreement that they would avoid topics of obvious vulnerability. Not wanting to be a party to this conspiracy, I asked him what vulnerability she protected in him, and found out that he still sucked his thumb when he slept. What I did with this bit of news is irrelevant. What is important is to see the rule, the expectation, that underlies this couple's tacit understanding: to avoid topics which would lead to exposure. The "parent" in this example possesses many different aspects: my client is free to behave in an infantile manner which goes beyond his thumb-sucking; his wife is free to kill herself. The parental rule, as we can see, is at best neglectful.

We can now rather easily turn our attention to sex. When asked, a married couple will frequently say that theirs is less than satisfactory. Why is it that a sex life can be so good before marriage and those first few months after the ceremony, yet become so routine and unfulfilling (as well as infrequent, of course) just a short time later? How can this wild and willing person become inhibited and unenthusiastic? The return of sexual interest after divorce, of course, demonstrates the emptiness of all those excuses marriage counselors often hear: "She never initiates sex. I'm sick of doing it myself," says a man who, after divorce, initiates sex as often as possible.

We all know that there is a taboo about having sex with one's sister (or brother) or mother (or father). When we have created our spouse in the image of a parent or authority, when we become children of the same parents in the pseudo-equilibrium, there arises an unconscious taboo which mimics the incest taboo. Sex—and the relationship—feels more intimate at the beginning, when the partners don't know each other, than later, when presumably they know each other much better. When the relationship animation has been repressed by the roles, rules and expectations we created and recreated, large parts of ourselves are suppressed as well. We are merely partial selves. To try to recapture those lost parts of ourselves is a violation of the rules, and a threat to the predictability and security of the relationship.

A Protestant minister once came to me for analysis. When he met his wife he was a student activist at an Ivy League university. A radical in the sixties, he was in the forefront of the sexual revolution of that era. He also wanted to be a minister. Once he became a minister, his attitudes about sex seriously conflicted with his ministerial persona. He recalled once, shortly after his ordination, wanting to have sex with his wife. He felt an inner conflict about his identity. He couldn't remember who he was. He thought, to himself, "Here I am, a man of God, meant to be pious. I want sex." Then an even more disquieting and intrusive thought occurred to him. Having been quite an active and uninhibited lover in the past, he suddenly thought: "She's seen me shit. How could she be seduced by a man she has seen shit?" This is a classic example of the inner conflicts between role, expectation and animating impulses which cause such problems in the sexual relationship. He wanted his wife to see him as ministerial. He wanted his wife also to play the role of the minister's wife. He also wanted to appear as a tempting seducer. And he knew she had seen him at his most exposed. He did not act, and they did not make love. Their sex life went downhill from there. We also have to ask why his wife did not say anything about their increasingly unsatisfying sex life. She obviously had her own conflicts; but the effect of her silence was the continuation of the pseudo-equilibrium in which neither dealt with the inner conflict giving rise to the problem.

Just as incest-taboos [1] maintain tranquility in a tribe or culture, the taboo in marriage preserves peace. If separation becomes imminent, both partners may tell their analysts how hard they worked not to rock the boat. They will not often realize, however, that this attitude is a major factor in their separation. [2]

Aggression in the pseudo-equilibrium seems to focus on maintaining those rules, roles and expectations we have erected. The aggression defends our right, if you will, to remain stuck. We do not see it as such at the time. The woman who would not tell her husband whether she was having an affair believed that she was defending her right not to be put on the defensive. We found out that the woman was in fact defending her right to be unconscious of her deep wounds. She is, of course, free to remain unconscious. No one will force her to look at her pain. On the other hand, her unconsciousness leaves her vulnerable to her husband, unable to differentiate herself from him. In this sense, this person found that her aggression served not herself, but her unresolved inner conflict, one side of which was a self-perception as a "slut."

A good marriage therapist will work hard to read the coded language in a marital argument. One must always ask why couples *want* to fight over trivial things. Couples can themselves sometimes see through the arguments to the underlying problem of psychological incest. Either way, with or without therapy, the equilibrium is disrupted and the real conflicts surface. For many, all we need do to resolve the problem is look to our parents' marriage. The conflict often remains repressed, however, and the marriage then becomes filled with bickering, periodic flare-ups, and only occasional moments of tenderness. But for the most part these partners will either divorce or live distantly-related lives, *1988 – ...?* looking more like companionable or not-so-companionable siblings than the lovers they once were.

ugh!

SEPARATION

yes

One of the most effective ways to differentiate ourselves from those around us is anger. Often, when someone we have been close to is leaving for some reason, we will get into an argument with him. Argument has a way of pushing the other person away from us, so we may see them more clearly, so that we may see ourselves more clearly, so we may defend ourselves from the other. In any event, the immediate effect of anger and argument is separation (paradoxically, those who have stayed with a painfully long argument to resolution often report an intense feeling of closeness afterwards).

The goal of the equilibrium stage, as well as the mutual repression and suppressions of the pseudo-equilibrium, is thus to avoid conflict. As we have seen, the avoidance of the real conflicts gives rise to conflicts which seem childish at best. The little arguments that couples have about garbage disposal and toothpaste caps serve to let off steam generated by the frictions which necessarily arise. In a pressure-cooker, if there is too much heat, not enough water, and inadequate ventilation to let off steam, the thing being cooked burns. It becomes black and unappetizing. The relationship—the pressure cooker—is liable to explode.

define term

The shadow has something to do with this business of falling in love. In fact, when the anima and animus are activated and projected onto the lover during infatuation, shadow contents are also projected. The shadow, composed as it is of personality traits which threaten or contradict our ego image, becomes a part of the beloved. As I mentioned in Chapter V, the possibility exists that we may actually integrate and live out some of the shadow personality traits activated by the projection of the anima or animus. We may expand our image of ourselves, enlarging as we do so our repertoire of perceptions and behaviors.

There is a reason, however, that some of these contents are repressed, since they can be just too threatening or too distant from how we want to see ourselves to be admitted into consciousness. We are left with

by letting down my defenses, e.g., incorrigible "wolf" / love bunny Bill; Fraser, the Lion

these projections as they appear in our spouse. The introverted man is terribly irritated by his wife's extraversion. He hasn't the faintest notion that he is irritated by his own repressed extraversion. He may, from time to time, feel self-conscious, even embarrassed the day after he had just exposed his extraversion to an unfamiliar woman he met at a social gathering. But he never links his self-consciousness with his irritation at his wife. She may try to help him see this by pointing out the obvious similarity of their behaviors, i.e., "What about that night you were coming on to the little tart at the Smith's?"

Shadow contents which have not been integrated into and expanded consciousness are repressed and projected onto the spouse, who also carries, confusingly enough, the image of the authority who holds us down and limits our expression. We no longer are able to differentiate ourselves from this other person. We are both trying to live by the same rules, so we look alike. We are projecting the unwanted contents of our own personality onto the other, and then complaining about them. Add to this any pressure from our jobs or other life situations which we do not talk about with our spouse. Depression, anger, resentment, fantasies of separation (escape), loss of self-esteem, all of these describe the blackening that is taking place in the pressure-cooker.[3] The effect is an impulse to throw the thing out, to separate, to be rid of this person we used to love, but who has changed into a monstrous distortion of all the things we thought we were rid of when we fell in love, left our parents' homes, or separated from that earlier ill-fated and equally horrible relationship with that other person who did exactly the same things this partner has come to do. We are angry, we are hurt, we are disappointed. But most of all, at this point we are in a hurry. All the repression has broken down, the partner looks horrible, we are in immense pain. And all we can think of is how to get out, to find another life, with or without someone new. As one client said, "just give me some relief!"

DREAMS

Up to this point we have not seen the unconscious side of the problem of the blackening and the separation. A colleague of mine, now dead, generously gave me permission to use the dream I am going to present first. The dream so clearly described the psychological situation I am discussing that he felt it important to ask his analysand for her permission. She was a thirty-five year-old woman, an architect, who had lived with her lover (John) for more than five years. She had this dream several months before she sought analysis with my colleague, and had been so disturbed by it that she wrote it down.

> On the way to the office, the usual road, I'm driving through the reed of the wildlife preserve. Suddenly the street runs into the swamp. Without noticing I drive into it. When I begin to realize what has happened, the tires begin to sink deeper and deeper. I can't open the door anymore. I feel immense anxiety but no panic. I am fearing the end. Suddenly, at the edge of the swamp John appears. He makes the greatest effort to draw me out of it by laying planks, but the mood (sic) was rising higher and higher. I noticed that all his efforts are failing. Suddenly the mass of the mood (sic) is in and on my body, and around my neck. It rises into my nostrils. I still can see John's desperate gestures. He shouts: "Doris, I can't help you!" I sink down.

While this dream graphically represents the blackening (*nigredo*) I describe in Endnote Four, it also signals that the dreamer's relationship is in serious trouble. The car and driving represent an identification with ego-images associated with the prevailing spirit. In the past, horses were the primary means of transportation and represented a rather more natural source of energy available to consciousness, namely the instincts. In our mechanized world the automobile has replaced the horse, and the ego has replaced the instincts as our primary orienting point. No longer connected to the earth and nature, we are freed from one kind of reflexive response, the instinctive, but become bound to another form of automatic response, which is the identification with a prevailing spirit.

Creating as it does a more tranquil lifestyle, we can immediately see the benefits of identification with the prevailing spirit. Much more difficult is to see the long-term effect of the repression of the instincts. To the extent that the ego has been able to overcome instincts, we become, but only in a limited sense, masters of our own fate. The dreamer, an architect in steel and glass, designed and planned projects which were elevating and modernistic. Her analyst told me that her work seemed to deny nature, to extol the virtues of austerity and asceticism (as well as, of course, estheticism). Since the dreamer is on her usual road to work, it seems her life has become routine. Her life has become rutted by her lack of vitality and connection to the instinctive world. From the discussion on equilibrium, we know that her loss of instinct is directly linked to the prevailing spirit, the professional and personal virtues with which she identifies. In the dream, the psyche compensates the one-sided identification by reaching out and grabbing her. The natural and instinctive aspects of her personality erupt, in her outer world, as depression, loneliness, dissatisfaction with her lover, anger and hopelessness. The inner world represents this as the road leading her into the swamp. A driving ego creates a two-dimensional world devoid of instincts. This alienates her from her grounding, to which she is powerfully returned when the depression and loneliness overwhelm her.

When the car sinks into the swamp, the dreamer is no longer insulated from nature, but rather is at its mercy. Her failure to pay attention to her perceptions, feelings and attitudes, her denial of the reactions and needs which contradicted her identification with prevailing spirit, now erupt as powerful affects over which she has no control. For this dreamer, sudden outbursts of anger, periods of depression, and fantasies of separating from her lover were becoming frequent. During this period (which the alchemists called the *nigredo*,[4] and which I am calling the blackening), the partners can no longer trust themselves to behave in a predictable or compassionate manner. The partners are subject to more frequent instances of anger, guilt, bitterness and hurt. As in the dream, once the person becomes mired in the black swamp she cannot escape; she cannot just open the door and leave.

To escape, the dreamer would have to roll down the car window and allow for the pressure to equalize. The dream image is useful because it reveals so perfectly that physical laws can metaphorize psychological experience. Doris cannot escape because what had been a state of equilibrium becomes a state of disequilibrium from which she cannot escape until she is overwhelmed by its affects. The equilibrium she created in the outer world is mirrored by a disequilibrium in the inner world. Her adaptations to John, her career, her social circle and culture create equilibrium externally, while her inner world decays and rots. The repression of reactions and needs which conflict with Doris's ego-image, her prevailing spirit, causes a disproportionate amount of psychic energy to remain unconscious, unavailable for use in the outer world. She can feel no animation, nor can she have much energy to change things. And she cannot escape so easily: she must wait until she is completely overwhelmed—in the dream world, until her car is filled with mud—before she can leave.

I think it likely that many marriage therapists will recognize this situation from their own practice. There are couples who come to us who seem beyond help. We may refer them on to other professionals, believing that the problem is a mismatch of therapist and client. We may recommend that the couple divorce, because we can see no good will between them. They seem absolutely determined to kill each other emotionally, and have no apparent desire to face themselves. If we can see that the blackening is directly related to the repressions and adaptations which are necessarily being overthrown at this time, we may be able to develop the patience and distance from which we may watch the equilibrium dissolve into another form of relating.   *← OK*

We must now ask ourselves why John is so ineffective in helping Doris out of her dilemma. A combination of factors renders him impotent at this time, the most obvious of which is that *he* is her problem. In the dream, John is not only himself, of course, but also a representation of a negative animus. The negative animus, in this situation, is the prevailing spirit with which Doris has identified to her detriment, and which is projected onto John—who is thus the mean-spirited, power-driven authority that has ruined Doris's life. John's attempt to save Doris is paradoxically just what she does not need. If she were saved, she would, symbolically, just get another car, go to work and in the future perhaps avoid that particular road.

The depression and other feelings which arise during the blackening are meant to redirect Doris's life. John unconsciously conspires with Doris, for his own reasons, to maintain the equilibrium, by pulling her out of her depression. One can imagine that Doris was a real pain to live with at this point. That, and his desire to preserve the relationship which seems at this point to be in serious trouble, are his most obvious motives for making a bridge (the planking) to Doris. But the depression and the bitterness must be experienced if the relationship is to survive. In most marriages, however, the need for security and the fear of loss join hands to prevent the spouse from standing idly by while the other slowly sinks into his or her own swamp.

In this dream, the repressed instincts have reclaimed their birthright by dragging the ego into the swamp. The psyche seeks to right a disequilibrium by loosening the ego's identification with prevailing spirit. The relationship takes on the chaos of this inner struggle, with floods of shadow feelings and perceptions about power, betrayal and abandonment projected onto the partner.

One cannot claim that a particular pattern of behavior is instinctive, or a necessary part of human experience, from just one case study. Dreams like Doris's appear over and over again, with remarkably similar images, in the dreams of those who have consulted me over the years. Obviously I cannot present each of them, though I would like to show two more examples of unconscious images which reflect the blackening, and the marital situation they amplify.

The following dreams came from a forty-six year-old woman who had been married only six years. She had never been married before, while her husband, ten years her senior, had been married and divorced. He had also had several children, now adults. My client, Amanda,

E = critical spokesperson

No kidding!

Duh!

came from a large family and was the last of her siblings to marry, even though she was the third oldest of eight children. Fearful of becoming an "old maid," she felt intense conflicts whenever she met a man who was interested in her romantically. The right man finally came along, she fell in love, and married him.

Since she thought she was beyond child-bearing age, she talked with Carl about adoption and learned that he was opposed to having any other children. Amanda, a grammar-school teacher, was crushed, though she didn't realize it. A shy and passive woman, she adapted to her husband for several years, repressing her disappointment at being denied her lifetime dream of raising a child. She changed careers, found other outlets for her energy, and lived a relatively tranquil life with Carl and her friends.

Then, suddenly, one night she had a panic attack; she thought her whole world was going to fall down around her, that she was losing her mind. For days she was depressed, then anxious, then in panic, and finally she sought help. She went to her family physician, who examined her closely and found nothing with which he could establish a diagnosis. He sent her to a neurologist for a consultation, and still no organic pathology could be found.

After careful analysis it became quite clear that her panic, depression and anxiety were related to her marriage. Her first dream was of a man, a vagrant and criminal, who was trying to break into her house. This motif is quite common, not only indicating anxiety but pointing out its source. The vagrant, a pariah abandoned by culture and collective, represents an animus attitude contrary to the prevailing spirit. That he is also a criminal suggests that the animus attitude is a threat to the prevailing spirit; thus the forces of authority (repression) seek to capture him. In the dream, Carl does not feel threatened by this vagrant and pays no attention to him at all. Carl in fact cared very little about what was going on in Amanda's outer life. The dream reflected the outer situation rather well, although Amanda did not want to see it at this time.

After a year, Amanda began to think that Carl was really a problem for her. She was becoming angry with him, flouting his "authority," and beginning to do many things by herself which they would have done together in the past. She had grave reservations about her marriage, wondering and worrying whether it could survive if Carl did not change. She had the following dream, which anticipated the blackening which would soon envelop her.

I am to begin a journey with a number of other people. The leader is a tanned, hairy, muscular and huge man; and he is the only one who knows the way. He is willing to be our guide. We've agreed to pay him, but I don't remember what or how much. We begin our journey. He purposely gets far ahead of us; far enough that we can't see where he's gone. We run to keep up. I notice the worn footpath he must have taken. He's going to tantalize us the whole way. The landscape is alien. At one point the only way to go, he says, is to lower oneself down through an ugly, huge bubbling mud hole. One woman from the group has already gone into it. She's down below—I wonder if she's okay.

The bubbling mud hole of this dream is symbolically identical with the black swamp in Doris's dream. Whereas Doris was a "victim" of her psychic activity, this dream suggests that Amanda is a semi-willing participant. Her analytical work over the past year had been of some use to her, and the blackening in this dream suggests an imminent, analytically-induced *nigredo*. The difference is that Amanda was able to see that the criminal of her first dream might not be so bad if understood as a repressed part of herself. Having taken some strides to integrate this animus character, his form changes, and he becomes a more attractive participant in her psychic life. But even still, she is struck by the bubbling mud hole, which she must succumb to if she is to deal with her alienating adaptations and repressions. The most important adaptation, of course, is the repression of her sadness and disappointment about not being a mother. This grief is part of the mud hole into which she must descend.

The psychological separation is the turning point in the process of individual and relational dissolution, and offers the possibility of "re-membering," and so reunion. But it is also the point at which the couple is at the most risk of physically separating, acting out in the world a drama which is, for most people, an intrapsychic conflict. Even the most abusive marriage contains the kinds of intrapsychic conflict which leads a man to be so patently abusive, and a woman to continue living with him after his behavior has become intolerable.

There are obvious extra-psychic and sociological factors to be considered when a person in an abusive relationship reaches the point of psychological separation, not the least of which are financial. All of these factors are immeasurably important and yet one can become so narrowly concerned with them that one fails to see the intrapsychic conflicts lived out in the marriage, in effect leaving oneself susceptible to repeating the same conflicts in another abusive relationship.

When the relationship has reached the painfully empty point of psychological separation, something will change. The question is not whether a separation will take place, but rather what kind, when, from what, and for what purpose. The mechanisms of control, repression

implication, it doesn't pay to wait for improvement

and suppression serve their purpose in creating a stable marriage, but they restrict other personality traits from being expressed. In all marriages the time comes when the individual emerges, at least unconsciously, from the parental and cultural prevailing spirit. Like a hero taking a dead king's place, the psyche produces a new direction even as it produces blackening and separation. The new direction, personified *term* as an anima or animus fascination in our dreams, sharply contrasts the blackened image of the spouse and the pain in the relationship.

A thirty-five year old Swiss woman came to me for analysis prompted by the feelings of insecurity she developed after her husband had begun analysis with me several weeks earlier. It is highly unusual that an analyst will see a couple separately, but for reasons which are not relevant to this discussion, I decided to take her on as a client.

Their marriage was in serious trouble. In a state of what we might *coming* call a desperate pseudo-equilibrium, each was frightened of emerging = *out* from identification with the other and the parental images. The tension *out* * in the relationship manifested itself in the form of Kristine's reflexive vaginal muscle constriction, which prevented intercourse, and Robert's loss of motion in his right arm. Robert was a painter, so this was a catastrophic occurrence. Both had been examined by medical doctors and found to have no physical problems. The couple came separately, twice each week, on different days, in order to minimize as much as possible the contamination which might result from working with the same analyst. After seven months of analysis, during which Kristine experienced a range of feelings about her marriage, the psychological separation broke through in a torrent of anger, hurt, resentment and *OK* disappointment.

Like the clients mentioned above, Kristine could imagine no way of containing the powerful affects erupting in her. She had the following dream, typical of this psychological stage:

> I am in student-type housing, in a fairly small room. There are two well-groomed women there. Robert starts dancing with one of them, and when he starts kissing her I think "that's that," and am angry, and leave. When I return Robert is no longer there, which doesn't bother me at all. I dance with someone who says he is an ear-kissing specialist, which he demonstrates. Then we are in another house, which looks great. . .

The two well-groomed women represent shadow elements that the dreamer had repressed since her college days, when she met Robert. They represent typical, old-fashioned images of woman. She had rejected these attributes at that time because they interfered with her adaptation to the masculine world. Her sexuality, however, was emerg-

* fear of the outcome, the result of the new direction

ing then as well, and she was becoming quite interested in men. As I
already noted, the tension between Kristine's masculine outer world
and instinctive inner world manifested in her reflexive vaginal muscle
constriction. Kristine claimed that "Robert wants a traditional woman,
and tries to make me into one." Robert could now be discarded, if you
will, because he had become, according to Kristine, the *embodiment*
of the traditional image she felt so desperately threatened by. She was
no more a traditional woman than she was a man. For reasons which
will become clear later, however, Kristine was caught in an inner
struggle in which her only images of personal identity were to be a
traditional man or a traditional woman.

Having rejected the image of the traditional woman, and attributed
the cause of her own struggle with the traditional woman to Robert,
she now blamed him for her feelings of being stifled and unhappy. She
began to fantasize about other men and of separating from Robert. The
dream described these longings. The "ear-kissing specialist" is clearly
a heroic but also sexual animal. The dream represents her fantasies of
sexuality and aggression. What has happened is that her animus has
split in two. Robert has become a personification of the prevailing
spirit: he is closely identified with the equilibrium, much like the image
of John in Doris's dream. Many of Kristine's repressed personality
traits have been projected onto Robert. To Kristine he now looks like
a conventional man who wants a conventional woman, and is trying to
make her into one. She had convincing evidence that this was true, as
do all people who are in this state. She could cite all those thoughts,
feelings and attitudes Robert displayed which supported her contention
that *he* was the problem.

The "ear-kissing specialist" represents the other half of the split
animus. He embodies the animating energy associated with the repressed essential spirit. While the relationship had contained this animation during the infatuation (and, the world "outside" seemed threatening), the reverse is now true. Salvation does not come from the
relationship but from separation. The barrenness once associated with
the everyday world is now projected onto the marriage.

The splitting of the anima or animus image is a symbolic representation of the individual personality emerging from the equilibrium, and
the emptiness of the identification with the prevailing spirit associated
with the blackening. The splitting of the contrasexual image is a typical
dream motif indicative of the archetypal process of individuation. The
dream motif of the split anima and animus can be seen as either the
expression or the cause of the psychological separation; but regardless
of its origin, it is a common experience during this phase of a relation-

ship. For example, a thirty-two year old analysand, Hal, married for
five years, and who in the outer world fought constantly with his wife
(Nancy) had the following dream:

> Nancy, Bill and I are in the same house. Nancy and Bill are in the
> bathroom together. There is a smoky glass window in the door and I can
> see shadows through it. Bill has taken a shower and Nancy is in a bathing
> suit. I am feeling mistrustful and as I walk by I look in there. I see them
> making love on the floor. I pound on the door at once, and open it up.
> They are lying on the floor, and Nancy gets up. I am enraged and tell
> her so. She says that the relationship has not progressed very far, but
> that it is deepening quickly.

Once again we can see that the spouse is associating with a shadow
character. The dreamer literally sees their shadows through the smoky
glass. The similarity with the previous dream lies in the relationship
between the spouse and a shadow character, Bill, for whom the dreamer
has mixed feelings. Anger is also a common trait in these shadow
dreams, as is a sense of insecurity. The sexual content of the dream
suggests that the instinctive side of life is involved in the insecurity. It
is clear in this dream, as well as in Kristine's, that the spouse is having
an affair with another part of the dreamer's personality, and that this is
threatening the dreamer's conscious standpoint. Several days later Hal
had a dream in which a new anima image appeared.

> I call for Diana at her home because I want to ask her out for a date. I
> feel embarrassed and ashamed while I am talking to her.

Diana represents the new anima image, the other half of the split.
Nancy carries the dreamer's shadow while Diana carries his animation.
The shame and embarrassment which Hal feels is related to the fact
that Diana, was, at that time, thirteen. Psychologically, Hal was also
thirteen in some respect. He is horrified that he, at thirty-two years old,
would fall for so young a girl.

Another example of the splitting of the contrasexual image is the
dream of Gretchen, thirty-five and married for four years. The inflated
image that she had of her husband had caused her to make compromises
that had seriously undermined her inner development. When she became haunted by doubts about her husband, she fended them off with
a vengeance. Finally she began to succumb to the doubts, and fell
into a depression which eventually erupted into the kind of one-sided
hostility which we come to associate with psychological separation.

> I am having an affair with another man. I feel as though I know him
> well, that he must have been in other dreams. He is in the theater, in

some back-scene sort of way. But he is very important to the production. I go to a production of the group with Frank [her husband], and I see that Eileen is in the play. Frank does not appreciate the play, which disappoints me. I like it, and after it is over, I go to see the other man. He is waiting for me. First he teases me that he doesn't have time to see me, but when I kiss him and act indifferent to his game he laughs and hugs me. We kiss and I feel incredible passion and love for him. We talk about our future together and he asks about Frank. I tell him it is very hard but I feel so strongly that I have to be with this man. He tells me that I have to leave Frank.

As in the other dreams, there are four characters, two masculine, two feminine. Just as we can see that there is no anger in the dream, there is also no apparent relationship between Frank, the dreamer's spouse, and Eileen, Gretchen's friend and a shadow character in the dream. The absence of anger reflects a lack of connection between Frank and Eileen. This dream, in contrast to the others, seems to be the harbinger of the psychological separation, suggesting that the splitting of the contrasexual image *precedes* the angry eruptions, at least for this dreamer. To Gretchen, Eileen represents an aggression which had been quite frightening to her. Eileen's marriage contained the kind of angry venom that Gretchen had been trying to ward off for several years. Now it loomed very close. The dreamer is impelled to look outside the marriage for satisfaction.

When the contrasexual image has split, with the animating image directed away from the marriage and the prevailing spirit identified with shadow traits projected onto the spouse, it is easy to see how people can decide to leave the marriage. Anyone who has experienced the pain and anger of a separation knows how convincing can be the evidence that the spouse is the problem. We think that if we can just get away from him (or her), if we can just find the right job, if we can just find the right person, then we will be all right. We forget that our spouse was, once upon a time, the right person too.

Marginalia (left margin, vertical): In is this my fear of provoking & vehemence?

Marginalia (right margin): boss / man.

Marginalia (below paragraph): * E's pride in changing jobs, not husband, ended in Davis.

REMEMBERING

At the beginning of this chapter I described a client who refused to tell her husband that she was not having an affair. We have traveled far afield from that point. I have presented material on the equilibrium, the pseudo-equilibrium, the repression and control which create them, and the blackening and psychological separation which destroy them. As we have been able to learn from imagining the pain of the outer relationship and observing the dreams in the inner world, the lack of differentiation my group client exhibited is the inevitable expression of inner psychic processes. It may seem unimaginable, but one can find a way out of this painful situation, to come to a different relationship with the same spouse, one allowing for identifiably discrete personalities as well as satisfaction for both.

Throughout this book, I have described mechanisms of repression in connection with the development of personality (Chapter III) and of marital equilibrium. Repression is nothing more than the act of forgetting who we are and what our reactions to life have been; the apparent goal of psychological separation, however, is remembering. With the eruption of affects come memories: of good times with and without the spouse; of bad times, mostly associated with the spouse; of activities not engaged in for so long; of aspirations long since forgotten. All of these memories arise like spirits out of the dismembered carcass of the marital equilibrium, swooping around us, haunting us as fantasies too frightening to heed but too powerful to ignore. = Co- See ? s

Ugh!...
but true.

The remembering process connects our present marital problems with the rest of our life. It puts marriage in context of who we are and are becoming, but also who we have been and where we have come from. We begin to define ourselves—we begin to see where we end, what are the limits of our personalities, as well as of our possibilities. By extension, if we can see where we leave off, then we can see where someone else, our spouse in particular, begins. Neither differentiation nor integration brings, in and of itself, a harmonious conclusion to one's inner work or a harmonious life with one's partner. Harmony and bliss are not the end-products of inner work. Passion and consciousness are.

ok

Regardless of what we do, remembering occurs during the psychological separation—which is a transitional state, a psychological end of repression, heralding the beginning of differentiation and integration. We can control whether the remembering is conscious or not and whether we attach any meaning to it. But remembering occurs as an autonomous act of the psyche, an expression of the Self, whose apparent goal is psychic balance. The need for balance arises out of a one-sided identification with prevailing spirit, the hallmark of the equilibrium— or rather, as we have seen, of the pseudo-equilibrium. Like scales out of balance, too much attention has been paid during the equilibrium to how life should be, who we and our spouse should be, and not enough attention paid to how life is and who we and the spouse are.

thank God

that bad word

With the splitting of the anima and animus in the psychological separation, the positive aspects of the contrasexual figure are projected

How unfair.

into the world as a fascination with a career, a new infatuation with another person, a religious conversion, or any number of other possibilities; the negative aspects, meanwhile, are projected onto the spouse. While the world seemed threatening during infatuation, during the psychological separation the spouse appears as the threat. We have what Jung called an *enantiodromia*—the thing has turned into its opposite. What was positive is now negative, and vice-versa. When the anima and animus are projected, as they are both in the infatuation and psychological separation, we have immediate experiences of essential spirit in opposition to the prevailing spirit. The fascinations of the psychological separation are also experienced as essential spirit, just as they were during infatuation. The tension between essential spirit and prevailing spirit was resolved during the infatuation by the predictability and security of the equilibrium. *Pain* is what prevents the ego from recreating an equilibrium out of the psychological separation, much as it created equilibrium out of the tension of the infatuation.

Change is the inevitable consequence of the pain experienced during this stage, but what that change entails depends entirely on the conscious involvement of the individual in his own drama. I doubt very much that we would get any argument from any therapist or analyst about the psychological results of entirely repressing the conflicts of separation. The personality would most certainly change, becoming more rigid and narrowly defined, with greater resort to anger and withdrawal as a means of dealing with life's problems. One would expect to see more intolerance of others, and more grandiosity about oneself. On the other hand, one might see depression as an expression of rigidity of personality, or compulsiveness, or a number of other neuroses. When the psychological separation erupts, it is very difficult and painful to entirely repress the feelings and thoughts that come to haunt us. Some people do it, but others leave the marriage, following the positive projections of the split anima or animus into the world with the same abandonment that marked the infatuation. I think we might agree that such people will once again be disappointed by whatever new fascination *if* they do not remember who they are and where they came from.

Pain is the factor which differentiates psychological separation from infatuation. All the elements are activated in the same way: shadow, positive and negative anima or animus are projected; essential spirit collides with prevailing spirit; personal history and intense feelings come to the surface. The longing for relationship, and the instinctive expressions of sexuality and aggression, push us and pull us. Gone, however, is the euphoria which made the tension bearable until the equilibrium smoothed the relationship out. In its place are hurt and disappointment which demand action, change, and understanding in order to alleviate our suffering.

During infatuation we fill in the blanks of our own vision with good will; in the psychological separation, these lacunae begin to harbor our ill-will.

= a warning: Don't repress the conflicts of separation—being in denial.

± Admonition: Do remember...
But after 40 years, can I trust my memory? See p. 146 *

NOTES

1. The patriarchal mandates which prescribe the perceptions, feelings, and attitudes of the couple translate into behaviors which limit personal expression in the relationship. The identification with prevailing spirit as a means to solidify the relationship hardens into rigid roles and stereotyping; this squeezes energy out of the relationship. The hardened prevailing spirit, now rigidly patriarchal, becomes the personal/cultural parent of which the couple are the children. The couple, now brother/sister, then mother/son or father/daughter, live out the incest taboo by prohibiting certain behaviors, feelings and perceptions which would seem to unsettle the general well-being of the "group." In the Endnotes to Chapter V, I quoted Jung discussing the *coniunctio* and claiming that the initial union has an incestuous tinge. Jung goes on to say:

> Incest symbolizes union with one's own being, it means individuation or becoming a self, and because this is so vitally important, it exerts an unholy fascination—not perhaps, as a crude reality, but certainly as a psychic process, controlled by the unconscious (*CW*, 16, p. 218)

Jung seems to be saying that the incest serves the purpose of recouping what belongs to oneself in order to know oneself. In point of fact the equilibrium and the consequent psychological incest create just this situation. All of the psychic ingredients are present during the infatuation and after; they are, however, projected. The apparent goal of psychological incest is to project onto the other what we do not see in ourselves, in order to reintegrate it later. If one can understand that the prevailing spirit, anima (or animus), shadow, and so forth, all belong to oneself, one will realize one's image of the "other" is an image of oneself. The compromises we make with our spouse are actually compromises we are unconsciously making with ourselves through our spouse. Again, Jung describes the apparent purpose of the incest motif:

> . . . on the psychological level, the tangle of relationships in the cross-cousin marriage reappears in the transference problem. The dilemma here consists in the fact that anima

138

and animus are projected onto their human counterparts and thus create by suggestion a primitive relationship which evidently goes back to group marriages. But in so far as anima and animus represent the contrasexual components of the personality, their kinship character does not point backward to the group marriage but "forwards" to the integration of the personality, *i.e.,* to individuation. (*Ibid.,* p. 230)

The unconscious projection of the anima and animus represents the potential for psychic movement. Knowledge of the contrasexual image *within* the individual cannot be attained until that image has been first projected onto a lover, or into the world.

2. The couple is a union of roles and images, their individuality repressed with their animation. The functional aspect of the contrasexual component, as mediator between conscious and unconscious contents, remains intact, and projected onto the partner. A forced marriage between the contrasexual mediatory function and shadow takes place. The spouse carries not only the mediatory function but also the shadow trait. The trait becomes negative by virtue of the ego's attitude about and reaction to it. Since the anima/animus functions as a conduit through which consciousness comes in contact with the unconscious (including the shadow, the instincts, and the archetypes), the mediatory function extends beyond the personal realm to the archetypal, collective unconscious. The spouse becomes confused with the archetypal and instinctual contents which we all possess, the negative mother, the rigid father, aggression and control, infantile reactions, and so forth. And so we have considerable evidence of the negative personality traits in the other, but without a corresponding vision of our negative traits. This is the nature of projection. The progressive purpose, as I have already mentioned in the discussion of psychological incest, is the later integration of these contents.

A hardening of positions is taking place in the marriage, the *calcinatio* I described at the conclusion of the Endnotes to Chapter V. In order to defend against the intimacy which would arise out of a thoroughly insecure relationship, the ego adopts a position, a standpoint from which it can put unfamiliar events in perspective. Not knowing who exactly our lover is, we look to old perceptions to understand what is going on. The old defenses are reinstated, the ego perspective hardens into a rigid standpoint, pain and joy dry up, and the relationship becomes stale.

3. Through the mechanisms of repression and suppression, the ego loses its connection with the vitality of the psyche, the anima or animus, shadow, and other contents of the collective unconscious, the archetypes and instincts. Left to their own devices, these contents work against the ego, compensating the one-sidedness of the dry ego standpoint. The ego is then attacked from below by the repressed contents. The marriage loses its positive character as the anima and animus are lost. The contrasexual component then is contaminated by or "wedded" to shadow, instinctual and archetypal contents which are either negative *per se,* or negative by virtue of the ego's standpoint. These contents erupt into consciousness as accusations, moods and other destructive behaviors. Characteristically, men have dark moods, negative fantasies, and outlandish sensitivities coming out of nowhere. Women will often have attacks of sharp criticism, intolerance, and biting sarcasm. It is difficult for an observer to understand what is happening when these attacks from below occur. The actors seem vastly different from their "normal" selves, and yet there is a kind of credibility to their argument or accusation that makes one take notice. After the attacks, however, guilt and bitterness generally surface, contributing further to the unhappiness in the relationship, and the confusion about oneself and the other. The relationship slowly, or suddenly, begins to die. The partners begin to feel a sense of doom, since their mates have become less acceptable. Earlier dreams and fantasies do not come true, and the partner is not what he or she seemed to be when love blossomed.

In alchemy this is the stage of *nigredo*. Also called *mortificatio, putrefactio* and death, it is considered by some alchemists to be the true beginning of alchemical work. This stage assumes that a soul is embedded in the stone, or the body, and that it must be freed from its bondage. In the initial *coniunctio*, the soul, i.e., the anima or Eros, is activated and wedded with the partner in an unconscious relationship. The merging of the contrasexual component with the partner is the first *coniunctio*, in which the soul and body are united. Body does not mean only the outer world of the lover, however, but also the body of the individual, so that instincts are activated in the individual and also projected onto the partner. In this sense, then, the body represents the instincts as well as the partner. Since the lover and the anima, or animus, are identical, a *coniunctio* of instincts occurs and generates the energy of the infatuation. The projection of soul (animation) into body has been described in many alchemical texts as well as in the mythology of the Kabbalists and the Gnostics. For example, in the cosmogeny of the Valentinians, Sophia was separated from the Pleroma because of her passion to know the creator, Bythos, thus creating the world as we know it—but only to be entrapped in it. In the Kabbala, the Matronit is separated from her brother/husband, the son of God, and is thrown into hell to marry the devil. She will be saved by the coming of the Messiah. In the "Song of Songs," the beloved is hidden in the stone:

> O my dove, that art in the clefts of the rock, in the secret places of the stairs, let me see they countenance, let me hear thy voice, for sweet is they voice and thy countenance is comely. (2:14)

The same image appears in the dreams of some analysands:

> I am standing in the water. There is a large man, perhaps twelve feet tall, swimming in a circle around me, with a very small man, perhaps three to four inches tall, on his back. I turn to look behind me and see a small blunt-nosed reptile swim past me with a fish sticking out of its mouth. The reptile swims to the shore and walks away. I follow it and find myself in a mansion, very old and very large. There is an old man who tells me there is a female spirit living in the wall. I put my right ear to the wall to listen, while the old man puts his left ear to the same wall, but on the other side of it, in a connecting room. I can see him in the other room because there is a mirror placed in the archway which provides access from the room I am in to the room he is in.

This was the dream of a thirty year old man who had been married for seven years. The female spirit in the wall is the anima projected into matter, that is, his wife, and now trapped there. The dream illustrates that the projection of the contrasexual component onto the spouse corresponds to the initial *coniunctio*. But the projection leads to repression of the energy, and the stagnation of the pseudo-equilibrium gives way to the slow death of the *nigredo*.

4. The *nigredo* represents the death of the soul/body marriage, and initiates the process of extracting the soul from the body. Psychologically, this extraction process corresponds to the withdrawal of projections and integration of their content—but not quite. The *nigredo* is projected back onto the spouse in such a way that he or she seems to be deadened. In Picture Five from the *Splendor Solis*, a black man emerging from a watery grave encounters a beautiful woman. The parable accompanying the picture says:

> The spirit dissolves in the body, and in the Dissolution extracts the soul from the body, and changes this body into soul, and the soul is changed into spirit, and the spirit is added again to the body, for thus it has stability. Here then the body becomes spiritual by force

V

of the Spirit. This the Philosophers give to understand in the following Signature, or
Figure: They saw a man black like a negro sticking fast in a black, dirty and foul smelling
slime or clay; to his assistance came a young woman, beautiful in countenance, and still
more in body . . . (Trismosin, *Splendor Solis,* Plate VIII and p. 31)

The picture and parable are remarkably close to the dream-image, excepting that it is
the dreamer's husband who appears, not the beautiful woman.

If we examine the parable closely, we find familiar thoughts expressed in its esoteric
symbolism. "Spirit" refers to conscious attention, the willingness to look at and expose
onself to the body, the unconscious; the body must thus be understood in all its
facets, including instinctual, archetypal, and shadow. Soul extracted from the body
corresponds to animation arising out of the unconscious. Translated, the text seems to

be saying that animation is the result of conscious attention to negative repressed contents; animation—in this case, negative animation—becomes our conscious experience (soul changes to spirit) and *is the expression of our instinctive boundaries* (spirit added to body, or instincts, for stability).

This is a remarkable statement. Quite literally, the parable says that eruption of dark feelings out of the unconscious brings about a stabilization of the conscious standpoint which is directly connected to our instinctive boundaries. The *nigredo* is the first step in that process, a negative animation which connects us just as intensely with the partner as had the infatuation.

In *Mysterium Coniunctionis,* Jung describes the torment of the alchemist during the *nigredo*.

> The *nigredo* not only brought about decay, suffering, death and the torments of hell visibly before his eyes, it also cast the shadow of its melancholy over his own solitary soul. In the blackness of a despair which was not his own, and of which he was merely the witness, he experienced how *it* [the Anthropos] turned into a worm and the poisonous dragon. (p. 350)

The alchemist is a symbol for the partner who is experiencing the powerful affects of the *nigredo*. The depression and bitterness which follow the dissolution of the equilibrium must be experienced if the marriage is to survive. The alchemist saw his work, and in particular the *nigredo,* as a process of spiritual transformation; the hardened ego standpoint is softened by the overwhelming affects of the *nigredo,* and the prevailing spirit becomes threatened by the emerging contents. In dreams during the psychological separation, this appears in the form of rampant insecurity.

The old prevailing spirit, and patriarchally rigid attachment to it, must die in order for a new essential spirit to emerge, one which is connected to one's own Eros and instincts. The ego must give up its attachment to those old ideals and images which produced the repressive and suppressive mechanisms of the equilibrium. Writing about the *nigredo* in connection with individual development, Edinger states that

> . . . the motif of the *mortificatio* [*nigredo*] of the king has an application to the collective psyche. Our collective God image [prevailing spirit] is undergoing *mortificatio* as indicated in the phrase "God is dead." The collective psyche is thus going through a *nigredo*. (Edinger, 1981, pp. 23–45)

In the *nigredo* of a marriage, it is not God but the prevailing spirit which is dead, and this deadness is projected onto the spouse.

The image of death in connection with prevailing spirit is expressed elsewhere as well.

> There comes about an inconstant fixation, then after a little the soft hardens. The watery becomes earthy and dry, thus a change of nature is made from one to the other; and then a single color in the form of a Black Raven, and the sulphur of male and female, have become of the same nature. (Jung, *CW* 14, p. 508)

The inconstant fixation is the infatuation. The watery image is related to the fecundity the infatuation seems to produce. The dry and earthy image corresponds to the *calcinatio,* and the Black Raven to the *nigredo*. The sulphur of male and female is related to the heat which dies in the equilibrium as passion dissipates. When passion has disappeared, the partners become indistinguishable from each other; they are of the "same nature." The head of the raven, *caput corvi,* blackened by nature, is another image of the death of the rigid prevailing spirit. Decapitation appears in the dreams of analysands, sometimes figuratively as loss of control, other times as a literal image. The following dream, of a twenty-three year old man, exemplifies this motif.

I am with Greg and we are going out somewhere. We are at his house, and we go to the kitchen to tell his wife where we are going. His wife is really my wife. We tell her we are going and she says nothing. As we start for the door she is in front of us, holding a sword in her right hand. As Greg passes she swings the sword, which cuts right through his neck. Then she calmly walks over to him and with such little effort opens the door to the basement; with her finger she flips the head off the neck and it bounces down the stairs. Then she closes the door, and we are standing there facing each other.

The dream describes both the *nigredo* and the *separatio,* which in alchemy are so closely linked that it is sometimes hard to distinguish them or to know which comes first. In any event, this dream shows that the anima, the dreamer's wife, is wedded to a shadow character, Greg, and yet it is he that dies. The friend represents an ideal with which the dreamer has identified, but also a shadow characteristic which he has resisted expressing.

In all the above dreams and alchemical passages, the prevailing spirit has returned to the unconscious, in the form of the swamp, the basement, or the alchemical bath. The apparent purpose of the *nigredo* seems to be similarly understood by Edinger, Jung, and von Franz:

> The shadow has come up with all those fantasies and impulses which seem so sinful and shocking to the Christian consciousness. The waters, which according to the text penetrate even to the lower hell, symbolize a loosening of the personality structure, a dissociation. (von Franz, *Aurora Consurgens,* p. 222)

This dissociation corresponds to the splitting of the contrasexual component, the anima or the animus. Religious mythology and alchemy abound with images of this split, in which the soul is freed from her bondage. In Valentinian Gnosticism, Christ, who was created by Bythos in order to strengthen the Pleroma, takes the corporeal body of Jesus, and eventually comes into the world to save Sophia from its devouring jaws.

The world and the individual ego have both lost contact with the Pleroma, the conscious Self. Jesus is the compensating image, the hero-savior of the Self, whose purpose it is to extract the soul from the grips of the world and the body. In this instance, the split between the world and the Pleroma is identical to the split between the unconscious and consciousness in the individual.

In the Kabbala, the King and Queen are son and daughter of God and his spouse. When Israel went into exile, the King was separated from the Queen. In one story the demon Lilith replaces the Queen as bride of the King, and he loses his power as a result of the separation. In another story the Queen is wedded to Shamael, the devil, and becomes identical to Lilith. The Messiah is the savior of the nation of Israel and of the King and Queen. Again we encounter images of opposition—King and Shamael, Queen and Lilith—with resolution appearing in the form of a savior-hero who frees the animation from its bondage in the unconscious.

In alchemy it is the essential spirit of the alchemist himself that comes into the world to save his soul from imprisonment in the body, in the world of matter. In the *Aurora Consurgens* the alchemist hears the lament of the anima:

> He that shall dig for me as money and obtain me as treasure shall not disturb the tears of my eyes and shall not deride my garment, shall not poison my meat and drink and shall not defile with fornication the couch of my rest, and shall not violate my whole body which is exceedingly delicate, and above all my soul which without gall is wholly beauteous and comely . . . (von Franz, *Aurora Consurgens,* p. 59)

In this image one hears the alchemist's soul crying out for salvation, its extraction from the unconscious, and its conscious recognition by him.

In the *Book of Lambspring*, Figure XIV (our Picture Six) shows the King in his bed after devouring his son. The text accompanying the picture says

> Here the father sweats on account of the Son, And earnestly beseeches God, Who hath everything in his hands, Who creates, and has created all things, to bring forth his Son from his body, And to restore him to his former life. (Delphinas, p. 303)

VI

The son is brought forth once again; father and son are reunited and become one. The son represents the animating hero-savior who would bring life into the world as the old king (prevailing spirit) dies. The son, as the image of essential spirit, is devoured (repressed) by a prevailing spirit that does not want to let go. Sickened as the personality becomes by the repression, it regurgitates the essential spirit lost in the equilibrium.

CHAPTER VII

REUNION

Our final topic of concern is the intrapsychic process of coming together, of reuniting the opposites of the psychological separation. The positive anima or animus figure that has emerged and split off (as a metaphor of the impulse to separate) ultimately brings the psyche back to the relationship and to the Self. As in the positive projection of the contrasexual component during infatuation, this figure acts as a mediator between the ego and the unconscious, introducing the ego to repressed parts of the personality. In the dreams presented, we will see, step-by-step, the encounter with the shadow, the parents and prevailing spirit, the spouse and negative aspect of the split contrasexual component, and finally the reunion of the split-off anima or animus. As we progress, we will see what can be integrated and what has been differentiated.

For those who have never been in analysis, it is difficult to grasp the mood, the humor of the consulting room and of the psychological work. Out of the consulting room, the descriptions of pain and insight, the memories and personal myths, seem ordinary and common. With this in mind, I will relate a dream which describes the drama of the psychological separation before differentiation and integration have begun. The dreamer is Doris, the young Swiss architect who had the "big dream" discussed in the last chapter. Doris was not yet in analysis when she had that dream; later she told my colleague that the dream had been powerful, but not sufficiently frightening to move her. She knew her

145

relationship was strained, but thought she could weather the storm by
herself. Then she had the following dream, which frightened her so
much that she called my colleague immediately, and thus began her
analysis. She had this dream three months after the wildlife reserve
dream.

> A journalist discovered an undeveloped film from World War Two in
> his archives. The enlargements he made showed the atrocities, the most
> unimaginable excesses of that time. A man in uniform is sitting in the
> chair with his legs slightly spread. A woman is lying on his knees. Her
> skirt is pushed up. You can only see her naked legs and her womb. The
> man is furiously cutting her womb with a big Bowie knife. The blood
> runs down her legs. In the other hand the man is holding a telephone
> receiver.[1]

Doris had separated from John before she had this dream, but she
associated it with him. In a simplified form, the journalist represents a
part of consciousness which "receives" the intense memories of the
psychological separation. Whether the memories themselves are actually understood by the ego is another story. Memories can surface in
vague, unformed ways, and be so threatening to the ego that they are
repressed once again.

In this case, Doris saw and was moved by images of sadistic brutality,
symbolic representations of her actual memories. In analysis, the dream
images began to emerge as Doris's own wounds. The film-archives
symbolized her unconscious, where memories had been "stored" because of their painful contents. Dreams of this kind are not uncommon:
castration dreams for men and slashing dreams for women often describe the intense struggle between prevailing spirit and instinctive
nature. There was a ritual quality to the slashing, the soldier's lap
becoming a kind of sacrificial altar. Quite literally, the dream-woman
is a sacrificial victim of Doris's identification with a rigid patriarchal
order. In order for Doris to achieve some psychic wholeness, this
animus identification must be broken; that is, Doris must become
distinct from the identification with this prevailing spirit, and see it for
what it is. The dream confronted Doris with the intense pain of identifying with the "Nazi" prevailing spirit, with the apparent purpose of
forcing her to see, and more importantly to feel, its effects on her.
Blood is the inevitable and painful prelude to transformation. But
we must differentiate the intrapsychic bloodletting which this dream
describes from the extrapsychic abuse which often is its substitute.

The avoidance of suffering one's own wounds is the surest route to
inflicting pain on others, especially those we are closest to. Doris knew

like a "gung-ho GI" in me ? The Nazis were my contemporary villans, too. ✗

that there was a "Nazi slasher" in her. And although we do not know in detail what happened during the analysis of this dream, we can imagine that Doris talked about how John had wronged her, as he well might have. But memories, if allowed to surface, inform us not only of the pain done to us, but also the pain we have wrought. This dream describes the process of remembering, the bleeding, the passion of the psychological separation. Getting through the anger and resentment to the hurt, disappointment and vulnerability being protected by instinctively aggressive responses must be left to later, when the ego and consciousness are more receptive to the gentler feelings. At this point in the drama, the Nazi who "cut off" Doris from her instinctive nature was now focused on John, in the form of accusations and intense dislike. John became the embodiment of this negative animus figure. In a figurative sense, however, the woman in the dream is not only Doris but also John's anima, both of whom have been terribly wounded by the Nazi, a symbol of the rigid prevailing spirit, anti-instinct and ✗ anti-nature.

Had we access to some of John's dreams over the life of the relationship, we might find a similar image: a woman dear to John who is being attacked. The image would express John's pain whenever Doris, in the *a tongue* midst of identification with this negative animus Nazi, goes after John *lashing* with a venomous verbal assault. Doris herself becomes the Nazi slasher, attacking John with the same vengeance with which she is being attacked from within. *Ugh!*

With a life of its own, the negative animus governed and dictated Doris's behaviors, perceptions and self-image. When the instincts emerge in the aggression and yearning for distance from John, the Nazi animus was projected onto John, who only "earned" a small portion of it.

i.e. deserved; misplaced aggression,

e.g. "You ain't the boss of me."

* * * * * *

In the psychological separation, the head, the intellect and prevailing spirit are overwhelmed by feelings and needs neglected once the relationship became secure. The split anima or animus image symbolizes the inner split, where aggression is directed at the spouse and oneself, while the need for relationship and sexuality is directed into the world. Once the anger is projected onto the spouse and deep wounds are revealed, the fiction of being a couple dissolves. The partners can no longer maintain the illusion that formality and conviviality are expressions of intimacy. Distance is increased by the projection of the positive elements of the split anima or animus image into the world or onto a new lover. The entire psychic standpoint becomes the mirror

Note chronology that = precondition for a new relationship ?!

the flip side

inverse of the infatuation. The relationship becomes the threat, and salvation comes from "out there," in the world.

The dreams I presented in Chapter VI illustrate that split and psychological separation—and yet, with the exception of Doris, none of the couples in question physically separated; each was able to imagine the split as a symbolic one. The individuals were able to see the anima or animus as a part of themselves which needed to be confronted and integrated.

The identical process occurs with couples who separate. After the initial euphoria or relief, many divorced people immediately seek a new relationship; others go back to their former spouses. In either event, the new relationship is a projection of the positive aspect of the split anima or animus image onto another person. The individual is still confronted with the task of uniting the opposites, of healing the split in the inner world.

The eruption of the instincts in the psychological separation and the bloodletting that accompanies it are essential if the couple is to create a relationship which more accurately reflects and expresses the totality of the respective personalities. This cannot occur if the partners remain identified with prevailing spirit; collective world views and behavior are only masks. The force of the ensuing dismemberment and bloodletting breaks the masks apart and reveals the individual behind it, in all his pain and folly. = also = pain of foolishness that E accuses me of,

Most of us know people who, years after they have been divorced, still feel a level of anger, hurt, disappointment and betrayal both disturbing and impressive in its duration. We expect people to feel intense emotions during separation and perhaps for some time afterwards. We expect a period of healing when we hear about the couple's problems, their rancor, their bitterness, as well as blame and even the hatred which propelled them out of the relationship. But after a time, if the divorced person does not forget the pain, we back off and don't even raise the topic. Either we get sick of providing support or are irritated by the acerbity, the maudlin self-pity. We ask ourselves why this otherwise likable friend or acquaintance continues to harp, years after the legal proceedings are over, on a dead relationship. We ask ourselves why he or she goes back to court year after year to contest alimony, child support, custody, visitation rights. We begin to wonder what exactly is fueling this continuing and apparently unhealthy passion.

To confuse the issue, we have recently begun to encounter the phenomenon of the friendly divorce. We know that any artificial equilibrium eventually dissolves into a psychological separation which releases bound-up and powerful affects. We also know that anyone

how to identify

* Hence the onus of being "the other woman."

*Oh, oh... cuidado**

who has only faked an amicable divorce will eventually be caught by
repressed affects anyway. We can thus concentrate on the persistent
emotional reaction, for two reasons: first, because a truly amicable
divorce presents no problems to be analyzed, and second, a faked
amicable separation will become a persistent emotional problem in any
event, either in reaction to this relationship or to a future one.

*time
* bomb*

Simply put, the persistence of the emotional reaction to a separation—whether the angry and bitter or the despondent and depressed
variety, or a combination of the two—is due to a conscious standpoint
unconsciously identified with the instinctive reactions of the psychological separation. At this juncture, it is important to keep in mind that the
anima and animus have a dual role. Content and function were merged
into the same image during the infatuation and equilibrium. In the
infatuation, the anima and animus were activated, and they brought to
consciousness other contents of the unconscious as well as the content
of their own complex. In the equilibrium, the anima and animus,
identified with and seen as the spouse, mediate the shadow contents of
the projector. When, for example, a wife carries a shadow part (e.g.,
extraversion) of her husband, she also carries the mediating functions
of the husband's anima, the content of his anima (emotions), and the
shadow (extraversion). The husband could be annoyed with his wife
for her extraversion, and yet be secretly pleased that she fills up the
quiet spaces in their conversation so that he does not have to.

collusion?

In the separation, the negative anima or animus carries the content
of the shadow and other negative images of the unconscious. The
spouse then becomes identical with the negative content and cannot
serve the positive function of mediating between those activated contents and the ego. The split in the anima or animus image raises the
possibility that the ego may follow the positive image, the savior figure,
and so become conscious of the constellated contents. The positive
anima or animus image is an unconscious compensation for the one-
sided negative image of the anima or animus merged with the spouse,
which is chained to the shadow and the instincts. Yet the positive image
of the anima or animus leads the ego back to other, ambivalent contents,
and thus generates more suffering as the psyche begins to untangle the
mass of projection and repressions.

?

not more ...!

People caught up in the same affects years after the separation
experience life as if time has not passed. The memories and affects are
expressions of the psychological separation, and they are as vivid as
ever. As I have already mentioned, aggressive affects are intended to
protect the Self, and the memories are activated to remind us of what
the Self needs to protect. But then something goes wrong. For some

OK!

reason, the ego, the conscious center of the personality, does not integrate what the psyche produces in order to heal itself. Rather, the personality remains split; while the anger (or despondency) persists, the wounds are all felt to be within oneself, while the ex-spouse carries all the blame. Yet it is also common for the despondent partner to assume all the blame, directing the aggression inward. One's depression then becomes fueled by guilt, a perception generated more by lack of self-awareness and reflection than by empirical psychic reality.

The development of the capacity to reflect is not unique to the separation process, though without it one cannot integrate what is brought to the surface by the psychological separation. Reflection requires inner vision undistorted by prejudices or prevailing spirit. The self-image of the divorced person who persists in seeing himself as victim and his former spouse as perpetrator of the wounds (or vice versa) is distorted by his prejudices of what is proper behavior, supported by the prevailing spirit, which may confirm or condemn his past behavior and thus leave his knowledge of himself and his world unchanged. Yet we cannot learn to reflect without reflecting on the need to develop the capacity itself. We need Self-knowledge to know that we need to develop Self-knowledge. It seems that pain is the impetus to the attainment of both reflection and Self-knowledge.

During the psychological separation, those who reflect on their marriages are likely to see a number of familiar problems and conflicts. We cannot have spoken in general terms about so many aspects of infatuation, marriage, equilibrium, disequilibrium, and psychological separation unless a similar psychological dynamic underlay them all.

We can now turn our attention to the dream series, which I use only as an example—in one individual—of the process which spontaneously arises during and after the psychological separation. The dreams will illustrate the process of confronting the split-off contrasexual component, in this case the animus. Out of that confrontation arise encounters with the shadow power-drive, the need to compete, the prevailing spirit, and the dreamer's relationship with her parents, which contributed to the contents of the prevailing spirit. The final dreams will describe the development of the reflective ability, which later bears fruit as compassion and renewed affection for the dreamer's husband.

DREAMS

The dream series I will present is a representative sampling of the unconscious material which the analysand brought to me over the course of nine months. We met Kristine, the dreamer, in the last chapter. In

early individual sessions, neither Kristine nor her husband Robert talked
about the relationship directly. They maintained a kind of friendliness
with one another, but did not relate to each other. The ear-kissing specialist dream disturbed Kristine, but she was also intrigued by it. For the first
time in perhaps years, she felt longing for a relationship—but not with
Robert. Instead her longing focused on Tom, a friend of the couple who
lived in their building. They had known one another for several years,
and the relationship had been merely friendly until around the time of the
ear-kissing specialist dream. Suddenly Kristine began to have fantasies
about Tom, disturbing but also satisfying images of them making love.
Dark feelings surfaced more strongly about Robert and his inadequacies,
making Tom all the more attractive to Kristine.

The first dream shows the positive aspect of the split animus, represented in the dream as Tom, bringing Kristine back to her relationship
with Robert, and also to a confrontation with shadow traits which she
has unconsciously projected onto her husband. She had this dream soon
after the ear-kissing specialist dream.

> I run a race on a beach with Tom. I'm flying over the sand, hardly
> touching the ground, while my feet are going in some sort of dance
> rhythm. I'm ahead by quite a long way. I come to a stream, where I
> stand puffing. Tom comes up and the stream is no longer there. I run on
> a bit and then lie spread out on the sand, puffed out.

Although Tom and Kristine were meeting regularly at the time of this
dream, there was no reason to believe that anything had changed in the
way Tom felt about Kristine. Kristine found excuses to see Tom because
she felt warmth and acceptance from him. The relationship was not
without tension, however. Kristine made several indirect attempts to
encourage a sexual encounter, but Tom seemed to be oblivious to them.
He liked to listen to her, she said, and seemed to value her feelings and
ideas. In this he was reminiscent of the man in the earlier dream, who by
virtue of ear-kissing symbolically valued listening and communication. *Oh! me too.*
Tom embodied the positive aspect of the split animus, and also may
have helped occasion the split by his presence in Kristine's life. The
mutuality of inner and outer reality is not clearly demonstrable. Was
the split in the animus image caused by Tom's presence, which presented her with an alternative image of what a man could be? Was the
split an intrapsychic reality first, and then projected onto Tom as a
means of making it conscious, and so manifest in her outer world? Did
the split and identification with Tom occur simultaneously, as direct
reflections of one another?

I was curious to discover why Kristine was racing Tom. She said

I'm relieved, Dosterian validates those 3 possibilities =ry-

Close // potential here.

there was a competition between them about what kind of relationship they would have. The competition was unspoken, and perhaps only felt by Kristine. She felt a longing for sexual union with Tom, which she saw him resisting. In fact, he may have been completely unaware of her longings, since she never let him know directly of her feelings. In any event, at the time of the dream she believed that she wanted to make love with Tom, and that he wanted only to be her friend and confidant. She didn't just come right out and tell him what she wanted from him, because she said she was afraid of rejection. With this answer, Kristine revealed her own inner resistance to a sexual relationship. Tom thus not only represents the outer man who may or may not want a sexual encounter, but also the inner Tom who wants the relationship to remain platonic. She had seen evidence of Tom's resistance to an actual affair—which was in effect a projection of her own resistance to acting out her sexual feelings with him. With regard to the strictly intrapsychic situation, then, the dream was saying that the ego wants to be in the lead, and act out the animation of the split animus in the world with Tom. The positive animus, on the other hand, lags behind, wanting to wear out the ego, exhaust it, and bring it to collapse, thereby stopping the race. Had Kristine been unconflicted about an affair with Tom, she would have raced after him and tried to wear *him* down. Instead, her own doubts about acting out the sexual fantasy wore her down until she collapsed. Certainly, Kristine's desire to act out the fantasy was in the lead, dancing and animating her all the while.

Once she became conscious of her own inner resistance to acting out the urge, she realized that the fantasy was an attempt to avoid dealing with Robert. This thought became clear as we talked about the next part of the same dream.

> Robert, in overalls, comes up to try the water. He goes in until he is wet to the armpits. I and a couple of other people are looking on, thinking he is crazy to get so wet in his clothes.

The dream clearly reveals the split image of the animus. Tom is the animating positive animus figure, while Robert looks the fool. Talking about the image of Robert wading into the water fully clothed, Kristine was visibly embarrassed. She hardly ever spoke about Robert in our sessions, and what she did say was quite neutral. Literally, all she could see of Robert in the dream was his right shoulder and up. The rest of him was submerged, underwater, unconscious. The people she was with were vague and yet appeared to share her thoughts that Robert was foolish. Since she was a member of a *group* in this part of the dream, we can imagine the others as symbols of her collective identification, her prevailing spirit.

Tom thus represents not only Kristine's outer world urge to remain platonic friends, but also, in the inner world, the positive animus which forces her into exhaustion. When she can no longer maintain the tension and collapses, then and only then does she begin to pay attention to the meaning of her feelings about Robert. Strangely, Tom's intentional or unintentional refusal to have a sexual affair with Kristine produced the collapse in which she could no longer maintain the illusion that she was in control. She then began to see that her feelings could not be dealt with in so cavalier a manner as having an affair. Since the positive animus image "intended" to compensate and oppose the negative image projected onto Robert, it would have been a defeat for the personality as a whole if Kristine had been able not only to win the race, [3] but also to master the positive animus. Had Kristine successfully outrun Tom permanently (i.e., had a sexual relationship with him), she would have continued seeing Robert as foolish and crazy. We cannot assume, however, that Robert is only an objective reality. He must also be a part of Kristine, because she became so embarrassed by him even as a dream image.

The water Robert walks into is important because it represents a kind of alchemical bath. In the Christian baptism, the initiate is symbolically or actually submerged in sacred water, whose purpose is to free one from the grasp of the devil and to provide for one's salvation. In the marriage Robert was associated with the dreamer's shadow or devil qualities. The value of this projection is obvious: it leaves the ego free of tension and darkness. By entering the water, Robert wishes to cleanse himself of the "dirt" projected onto him, and the dreamer's reaction is to belittle this. In Picture Seven of the *Splendor Solis,* this theme is taken up. The Seventh Parable to which the picture is connected states that

> Ovid the old Roman wrote to the same end, when he mentioned an ancient Sage who desired to rejuvenate himself was told: "he should allow himself to be cut to pieces and decocted to a perfect decoction, and then his limbs would reunite and again be renewed in plenty of strength." (Trismosin, *Splendor Solis,* p. 33)

Here, Robert represents not only himself, but the old prevailing spirit overwhelmed in the *nigredo* and torn apart in the *separatio.*

There is a secret connection, however, between the old prevailing spirit and the new essential spirit. This is represented by the new animus image, Tom, bringing the dreamer to the old animus image, Robert, who desires renewal. The new animus image returns the dreamer to the old, to watch as he immerses himself.

This immersion fails for a very important reason. As the above passage suggests, all the limbs must be immersed in the bath if they are to be reunited. However, the dreamer has not yet confronted all the "limbs," or repressed psychic contents. Only after the ego has confronted these contents individually can they be reunited in the bath. At this point the dream only presages the later process of immersion.

It is not yet at all clear who Robert represents, but as the dream goes on we begin to get some clues.

> Next, in a seaside resort hotel, Tom is chatting with a couple of young, not very clever-seeming girls. Then, to get rid of them, he says he has to ring his wife. He goes to the phone and rings up another woman in the hotel and pretends to be speaking long-distance to his wife. With this woman he seems to have a close relationship.

In the later part of the same dream, we will see Tom appearing rather amoral, that is, unconcerned with conventional morality. There is also a trickster quality to Tom which identifies him as a mercurial figure. He is as hard to pin down as the essential spirit he represents. For this reason the alchemists saw the need to "fix the volatile," which is to connect the spirit to the soul and body. Tom thus not only represents the mediating function which brings the dreamer closer to her unconscious psyche, but also the spirit which moves her.

As an embodiment of animating essential spirit, Tom represents such intensity of feeling that another infatuation must be posited to account for it. As in other infatuations, the animating animus figure is associated with shadow characteristics. The not-so-clever young girls are shadow aspects of Kristine; their infatuated schoolgirl crush on Tom reminded Kristine of her own feelings about him. The dream suggested, therefore, that a literal infatuation was not what was needed, nor a concrete acting out of the sexual fantasies. This is why Tom wants to be rid of the girls. In their stead, an unusually mature and attractive woman was on the other end of the telephone. We learn only later that this woman represents the possibility of a new relationship with the dreamer's own femininity. As we talked about this part of the dream, Kristine could not yet see that it was her own not-so-clever young girls which she saw mirrored in Robert's foolishness.

Although Robert had somatic problems (see Chapter VI), so did Kristine. Her tension and anxiety about the relationship manifested themselves as vaginal muscle contractions which made intercourse impossible. Her disdain for Robert and his symptoms left her free to forget her own problem. Now she had to face her own psychological condition, her own infirmity, which had been a factor in her coming to me in the first place. The dream brought Kristine to a confrontation with her own intrapsychic conflict, which she had so conveniently repressed by projecting foolishness and pathology onto Robert.

The final part of the dream helps tie up some loose ends.

> Then, there is another conquest of Tom's there. It seems that she came to the holiday place with orders from her mother to form a relationship with anyone so that her mother could move into their apartment and save money. I'm outraged that someone could be so conniving. Someone explains that this is the different morality of unintelligent people, and I should accept it with good grace. I do so, but inwardly I still feel angry with the girl's family, not with the girl herself, who no longer is there.

The stupidity which Kristine projected onto Robert was, in effect, *Oh!* her own. In a sense, she had been looking for a free ride in her relationship for years: a life free of conflict, tensions, and struggle with her own shadow. When we talked about the mother in the dream, some very revealing associations were made. In the first place, Kristine's mother was the first woman in her canton to graduate from university and be admitted to practice in her profession. This woman had obviously expected and received no free ride when it came to her professional training. And yet in her married life Kristine's mother was as conventional and unassuming as Kristine could imagine. In conflicts with her husband, Kristine's mother was manipulative and conniving, fearful that a direct approach would offend or provoke a touchy spouse. The seaside resort in the dream began to make more sense in context of Kristine's longing for a marriage which, in many ways, would parallel *car* the feeling tones of a vacation. The most enjoyable times in their *trip* relationship occurred when Kristine and Robert traveled. Quite literally, *valve* their marital problems were left at home. As Kristine became conscious *grinding* of her own manipulation, she projected the blame onto her parents, and more particularly onto Robert. If he were not so touchy, she would not need to be so manipulative. Here again we see pathology projected *pattern,* onto the spouse, leaving Kristine dependent on Robert to change if their relationship is to improve. *Sounds // to E's fears of my money*

The projection of blame often falls on the touchy, excessively sensitive, over-reacting, hysterical or abusive spouse. All of these character traits may be possessed by the spouse, but projection of the blame does not address the unconscious dependency revealed by the responsive indirect behavior. If Tom had been willing to have an affair with Kristine, she might not have had to face her marital problems or her own limitations. Although she could not grasp with any degree of depth what this dream meant to her, Kristine did understand that there was much more going on under the surface of her relationship with Robert than she had imagined. She knew that a connection was possible between her own physical symptoms and her feelings for Robert. She saw a contradiction between her mother's professional and domestic personality, and wondered about its meaning to her. She felt surges of anger at her mother, father and husband for *their* insensitivity towards her, and *their* demand that she adapt and accommodate them.

A short time later Kristine had another dream which helped her begin the process of sorting out the projections.

> Tom is sitting on the end of a bookshelf, next to my art supplies. I have the cloth in which I wrap my brushes in my hand. I hit down with this cloth on the end of my case, half on Tom's knee, saying: "it's my father's fault, it's my mother's fault, it's everyone's fault," hitting as hard as I can with the soft cloth for each person, smiling as I do. Tom says he also used to suppress the clown side of himself, and I laugh because this seems unlikely.

Kristine's dream thus helped her see the humor of her own reactions to the erupting emotions. Tom was a kind of supervisor or guide to comment on her reactions and provide an insight to help her endure the suffering. Of course, she was blaming everyone in the world but herself for the dilemma in which she found herself. The positive animus figure (Tom) helped her to see the humor in this, and not to take herself too seriously. The alchemists were intensely aware of the dangers of over-seriousness (heat). Too little heat and no transformation could take place; but too much heat at the wrong time could burn the material to a crisp and ruin any chance of creating something positive.

In the outer world, Kristine was feeling considerable self-consciousness about her unstable reactions to Robert and to Tom. The dream figure of Tom corresponds to a barely audible and not yet trustworthy voice in Kristine telling her to experience the affects but not to take them too seriously, as a final statement about herself, her parents, her husband or her marriage.

The emotions arising out of the psychological separation are powerful and moving in the sense that they create a shift in perception and behavior. If her positive animus feelings were enacted in the world, Kristine would have had an affair with Tom; yet by containing the urge to impulsively satiate an intense hunger, she was unconsciously thrown into the pressure cooker of making sense of her own feelings and perceptions. The danger of too much heat, that is, of being consciously over-identified with the suffering, is that the contents will burn up and be useless. The humor Kristine saw in the dream relieved some of the pressure and brought her to a vantage point which was, paradoxically, both in and out of the experience. Had she been told, either by me or anyone else in her life, that she should not take her feelings so seriously, she would quite naturally have felt that her emotions were being devalued, minimized. But when the dream animus said the same thing, symbolically, it was understandably much easier to hear, and thus more effective. *OK*

When we are infatuated, everything in the relationship has a seriocomic aspect. Blunders, gaffes and errors are serious because they make us feel self-conscious, but they are also comical. One of the first things to wane in a relationship is humor; and by the time a reliable equilibrium is created, humor may be confined to jokes and sarcasm, with little of the emotional flexibility that characterized the infatuation. For Kristine, this dream introduced a tinge of humor which took some of the rigidity out of her perceptions about herself, her parents and Robert. The clown image thus introduced the possibility of play, of emotional lightness in the midst of painful darkness.

Over a number of weeks Kristine talked about her early family life, remembering and integrating many incidents, emotions and inner experiences. She was by no means the product of an abusive home life. Her father was uneducated, but had made himself successful in business and agriculture. An odd couple, her parents had little in common. She remembered her father as a relatively rigid man whose expectations were implicit rather than explicit. She had to "read" her father to know what he wanted from her. Her mother, as I mentioned earlier, was a professional woman, cold and unrelated herself.

Kristine had few direct memories of her mother, but a significant one involved reading. When Kristine was seven, she was given a book as a door-prize at a friend's birthday party. The book was a children's story, one which any youngster might enjoy. Once Kristine returned home from the party, her mother confiscated the book, telling her that the book was not suitable for her. Instead she gave Kristine a classic novel well beyond her reading abilities. As we talked about the incident, Kristine recalled the shame she felt at being unable to read the book her mother had given her. She also recalled her confusion about why her mother had taken the children's book from her. She remembered, finally, the self-consciousness she felt in her mother's presence, wondering when her mother would next criticize her, and for what. As a seven-year old, Kristine's development centered around learning the rules, adapting to the world, and making her way in it. The memories of her parents and her recollections of the book incident helped Kristine identify the seeds of anxiety and insecurity which expressed themselves in her marriage.

Gradually, the prevailing spirit which had been Kristine's resolution

X professionalism related to/associated w/ coldness

XX Billy didn't get cookies when he hadn't learned his lines... + = love   I still don't bake or buy them!

of the anxiety and insecurity made itself known to her. She saw her self-consciousness as an inhibiting force that was identified with her mother's presumed perfectionism and rigidity. Her response to the predictable anxiety of being out of step with her mother was to identify with her and her values. She learned to concern herself with appearances, resolving the tension between the appearance she wanted to project to others and what she knew herself to be by "fading into the woodwork." Being as unobtrusive as possible was a goal which completely opposed her career goal, namely to be a performing artist. Underlying her self-consciousness was an urge for recognition which was expressed in her career choice. The negative image that she had always associated with her mother later was projected onto Robert.

A very complicated picture of Robert evolved out of these discussions. He became the idealized mother whose work was important, whose reactions to Kristine were overvalued, and whose needs were to be considered first. The magic moment for Kristine occurred very early in their relationship, at an art camp. They had just met, were deeply attracted to one another, and were also acutely aware of one another's talent. Kristine took a back seat to Robert, following his lead and subverting her own position in the class. Several years later, when the tension between Kristine's art and Robert's clashed in open competition, it was Kristine who adapted, choosing another medium altogether. When Robert began to develop his own symptoms (arm and shoulder troubles), the idealization began to break apart. She became, in effect, her mother, criticizing and devaluing Robert in the same way that she had always criticized and devalued herself.

The development of her own physical symptom, the vaginal contractions, served as an outlet for her unconscious anxiety and insecurity about her realization that Robert was not infallible. Once aware of this underlying problem, Kristine was able to feel her own sadness about losing an idealized love object, but instead gaining a human partner. She was not at all sure that she wanted a human husband because he would have human limitations which she would have to contend with. The next dream identified that fear directly.

> Robert is riding a small moped which belongs to my mother, with my sister sitting behind him. They are riding away from a store. I jump on the bike. Robert, who I now think is my brother, does not notice that I am also aboard, but remarks that it suddenly seems like hard work to keep moving. I announce my presence at this point.

This dream graphically illustrates the aptness of the expression "carrying a projection." Quite literally, Kristine's mother-complex was expressed in the image of Robert in the driver's seat of the mother's vehicle. Whether Robert was actually aware of this fact is irrelevant, as was his willing participation. The psychological incest of the equilibrium was a consequence, from Kristine's psychological standpoint, of her unconscious need to recreate Robert as the villain, the negative mother of her complex. First, she feared rejection and control, and thus adapted to Robert as she had done to her mother. The confusion was compounded by the presence of her sister behind Robert. This weak and conventional figure was another symbol of Kristine's adaptations, and when Robert turned into her brother, the psychological incest became clear. She and Robert became children of Kristine's mother problem, the unresolved tension which first manifested itself with Robert at the art camp. Her vaginal contractions prevented the incestuous sexual encounter which Kristine unconsciously feared.

OK, puts a damper on even married sex

We must, however, see Kristine's mother and mother-complex in the wider perspective of the prevailing spirit. The mother had to identify with the patriarchal world in order to make her own way in it and her chosen field. She had adapted to the world, submerging her own feminine nature and identifying with the more masculine Logos values of her professional world. In a very real way, the mother had to pass these values along to her daughter in order to confirm them, and repress whatever doubt about her own psychic state which may have shadowed her from time to time. Kristine recreated the mother's struggle not only in the professional world, but also in her marriage.

Awareness of the projections of the mother onto Robert helped Kristine begin to assimilate and integrate the powerful emotions that had such a stranglehold on her for the past several months. The dream suggested to Kristine that she might talk to Robert about what was happening to and in her. During the most intense period of the psychological separation, she had absolutely nothing to say to Robert, and what she did say to him was hostile, argumentative, and demeaning to both. Now she had something to say about herself, a fact reflected in the dream image, where she tells him that she is aboard and making the going tough. I did not have to tell her to talk to Robert because the impulse came from within her. The animation and movement was entirely hers, an expression of the natural timing and activity of a psyche that has begun to heal. Obviously, by talking to Robert she began to reveal to him some of the underlying conflicts and personality traits which she had been trying to hide from him these many years.

Awareness of the underlying conflicts is only a part of the solution, the reunion. Kristine still felt anxious and insecure, now for fear that Robert might leave her. Having projected shadow characteristics onto

+ concept of sick/wounded psyche

Robert, Kristine was in danger of leaving him. Having integrated her
tendency to manipulate and control him, she was now frightened that
Robert would be as disgusted with her as she was. The conversation she
had with Robert was more like a confession than a dialogue, and another
reversal took place. Robert became, once again, the carrier of the projection of Kristine's emergent image of psychological wholeness. If he could
accept her with these character shortcomings, she would be all right, she
thought, because she had not yet developed a psychological standpoint
that saw the *process* of individuation as important. So when she talked
to Robert, her fear of rejection centered on whether she was yet "good
enough" for him. Robert now carried the projection of her image of "good
enough," of psychological wholeness or health, because she had not yet
seen the value of being "in process."

After the conversation with Robert, which incidentally went rather
well from her perspective, Kristine had the following dream.

> I'm sitting with others around an improvised table, on improvised chairs.
> We are eating a meal. As we finish the meal a man appears in the
> distance and walks toward us. He is very tall, and clothed in a flowing
> full-length cape, and a black hat. He himself is very dark, with black
> hair, black eyes, and olive skin. He is an imposing figure. All the people
> recognize him and are on friendly terms with him. He looks into my
> eyes, and his eyes have a friendliness of mutual understanding.

Clearly, this man is another incarnation of the animating animus which
had also been symbolized as Tom and the ear-kissing specialist. He comes
back in this form in order to compensate for the one-sidedness of Kristine's projection of psychological wholeness onto Robert.

The dark man is the personification of Kristine's inner image of wholeness, connected to the natural world. He is dark and mysterious because
he is associated with the instincts and archetypal world of the unconscious. His darkness indicates that he is a connection to the chthonic
world of instincts and the matriarchal feminine. Later we will see that
he possesses magical qualities which enhance his psychic power and
authority. It is, however, quite clear that this animus is a positive figure,
very different from the Nazi in Doris's earlier dream. Both of the figures
are chthonic; this figure is a guide, whereas the Nazi personified the emergence of the negative affects of the *separatio*. The dream goes on:

> My childhood friend is there and is afraid of him. He asks if we, and
> especially my friend, have eaten anything which has been in a pressure
> cooker. One guy says yes, the beans and the turkey. The imposing man
> tells my friend she must get rid of it, she must vomit it up. He takes her
> into another room, and we hear her vomiting in rhythm to some music

he is playing. I go into her room and see her climbing up onto the top bunk in her underclothes. The dark man says to me that she will be alright now, she needs rest.

Kristine spoke fondly of her childhood friend, an outgoing, engaging little girl with whom Kristine frequently played. She had even been at the birthday party at which Kristine had received the children's book mentioned earlier.

Heidi represented Kristine's own social extraversion, so badly damaged when she was a child. We have already seen how her self-consciousness inhibited the flow of her natural energy into the world and manifested as the urge to blend into the woodwork. In a wholly unpredictable way, the book incident led to the repression of Kristine's natural development, and the loss of the kind of energy which she had seen in Heidi. More than just her social extraversion, then, Heidi represented Kristine's natural developmental gradient *before* it was sidetracked by the book incident. Heidi is therefore a symbol of the Self in its childhood, made sick by the pressure to adapt which first came from Kristine's mother and later from Robert. Instead of leading Kristine out of her marriage, the animating positive animus figure is leading her back to her earliest memories of herself and her identity, reconnecting (re-membering) her with the natural developmental gradient she had been estranged from for so many years. In the outer world, the pressure cooker represented the ideals she had identified with, her prevailing spirit. All of the "presses" then, became apparent: the suppression of her natural developmental gradient became repression, as she forgot who she was, and gave rise to oppression, which she first associated with her mother and then with Robert. Finally came the depression, the blackening described in the last chapter. The psychological separation threw off the "presses," releasing the energy bound up by the prevailing spirit.

The dream goes on, showing Kristine a road map of her psychic development.

The dark man and I are walking into the Olympic Games sport complex building. He takes a left side path and I take the right side path parallel to his. I think he has taken the wrong path, and that it will come to a dead end. I can see him walking along his path, and he is no longer so dark. He arrives where the path seems to end, but he keeps going. The path goes up and then down again. He walks under the path, stretching to his full height as the path reaches its highest point, and compressing himself as the path comes down again. I actually feel this feeling of being squashed together as I watch it happening to him. It is not very pleasant, and I wonder how he can bear it, as he is compressed to about two feet tall.

Kristine had the same questions many of us must answer during the anguished period of the psychological separation: what is the meaning of this pain? How much pain is too much?

The Olympic complex represents several different intrapsychic conflicts. In the first place, it symbolizes the enormity of the problems Kristine is facing, as well as her competition with Robert, which took various forms. The usual competition concerning their careers was overshadowed by a deeper and more unsettling problem: for Kristine, pleasure and satisfaction often came at Robert's expense. Seeing him as a fool was important to her self-image; awareness of this shadow-glee did not take her by surprise, since she had known about it for years. She hadn't taken it seriously as a problem, but had kept it hidden as well. When awareness of the trait surfaced, she felt quite embarrassed to have to admit that she was so petty. She could only see the problem in terms of her violation of a moral standard which said, in effect, that healthy people do not take satisfaction at their spouses' expense. Understanding of the complex, however, came from her admission of its presence in her personality.

The sports complex also represents the competitive, hierarchical rationality with which Kristine is identified. On one hand, she has internalized the collective expectations of women which forbids competition in the masculine world; on the other, she has identified with the collective masculine ideals of success and accomplishment. These two ideals have collided with one another and generated a painful conflict. For this reason she has to be prevented from eating the pressure-cooked food in the earlier part of the dream. This conflict manifested itself in the marriage as the dreamer consciously lived out the feminine ideal by mothering her husband, while secretly condemning him and competing with him in their respective professions. The left and right path represent the opposing ways of living between conscious and unconscious. The dreamer desires the straight and well-marked path of conventionality, while the animus shows her a vague and tortuous one. He is showing her her own unconscious nature, which is to be a mass of paradoxes: strong and weak, happy and sad, expansive and withdrawn. His path embraces the opposites, and compensates the rigid, rational and consistent road our culture expects and idealizes. Ultimately, she must incorporate the irrational way if she is to be freed of her identification with collective feminine ideals.

If we analyze Kristine's reaction to the emergence of the complex, we can see how it functioned and what its components included. Intrapsychically, a standard of behavior and personality had always existed to direct what Kristine should be. She inevitably fell short of those expectations, and so was forever in danger of feeling inadequate. She found solace in comparing herself with Robert, but only when he also fell short of certain expectations—i.e., his arm and shoulder problems. When the competition problem arose in her analysis, the complex took hold of her and she began to feel the shame and embarrassment which had driven the complex underground in the first place.

It is in this context that the remainder of the dream can be interpreted. The dark man was another representation of the positive animus, now also projected onto the analyst. A positive transference was the result, a not uncommon occurrence at this point in analysis. Out of the dream image of the dark man came a recognition of the two paths with which she was faced. She associated her own path with a rigid adherence to the ideals of her internalized prevailing spirit, which she called "being a dutiful daughter." The other path had always seemed to be a dead end, but, as she saw in the dream, it was in fact an alternative perspective on life. From the dream image, she began to see the possibility of relating to herself and her world in a new way, one which included personality extensions and contractions, emotional ups and downs, and serpentine detours from her own expectations and those of others.

The development of a new perspective for observing one's own psychological phenomena is a necessary outgrowth of the psychological separation. Whether this development is called a religious experience, a philosophical standpoint or a psychological insight, it is a concrete manifestation of the psychological separation, and heralds its approaching end. Out of the dismembered body of the personality arises a new spirit, a new understanding of oneself. From the blackness and bloodiness comes a cleansing, a whitening, which washes away the intense pain of the previous stage. And with the end of the psychological separation comes a glimpse of future reunion with the partner. Having been opposites for so long, the partners now realize the possibility of being on the same side.

Awareness of a new path does not, of course, translate into an immediate transformation of the personality. Kristine did not suddenly and completely integrate the meaning of the dream. My task was to embody the positive animus in order to help Kristine connect to the irrational parts of her which she had repressed—to help her begin to integrate them, test them, and finally to live them out in her life. After some weeks of talking about this dream and other associations, she had the following dream.

A fairly rich music student is in love with a handsome, sensitive and poor music student. They are always together, and want to stay that way. However, a very smooth, cultured man wants to marry her, and spends hours getting to know her father, until the father decides to let the man marry her. She refuses, but the father is adamant. The two lovers are very upset, and go for their last walk together before the wedding. At the wedding, which is a big ceremony, something happens which means that the wedding will not take place. The girl comes to my home.

The dream describes the tension between the ego (the dreamer herself) and the prevailing spirit (the father) over the wedding plans of the young lovers. Clearly, the young lovers are Kristine and Robert, who were in fact students when they met. The cultured man is the product of the patriarchal ideals represented by the father, a success in the collective world; he represents the idealized image of the desirable man with which she has identified for so many years. The dream seems to separate the dream ego from the young woman in order to create a relatively more objective vantage point on the interactions between the prevailing spirit, the idealized expectations which spring from it, and the true feelings buried under the weight of both. From this "whitened" perspective, Robert begins to seem more acceptable, and Kristine is able to see the effects of her identification with the patriarchal prevailing spirit. She can begin to imagine that many of the problems she has with Robert arose out of her idealized expectation of herself as a woman and human being, and her projection of these expectations onto Robert, both as persecutor (the dream-father) and as standard-bearer who needs to be cut down to human size (the cultured man).

The young woman is now allied with the real husband and opposed to the prevailing spirit which she had formerly accepted. As the psychological separation concludes and a new and more objective perspective develops, Kristine's image of her husband is separated from the prevailing spirit, and he and the old spirit can be seen for what they really are. By opposing the cultural ideals represented by the father, Kristine is able to effect not only the separation of Robert from her own father, but also to begin to integrate the loving feelings now identified with the bride in the dream. In effect, Kristine can begin to remember that she loves Robert, and why. By bringing the bride to her own home, Kristine has begun to understand and feel the animation, the passion, that had seemed not so long ago to be gone forever. But with it she also had to face the sadness, the loss of the old king, the patriarchal prevailing spirit which she had served so well in the past, and which had in return been her protection from consciously experiencing her own wounds.

The apparent goal of the psychological separation—to untangle the web of identifications between spouse, father, animus and shadow on the one hand, and between mother, spouse's mother and self on the other—brought about a complete revision of Kristine's perspective on herself, her marriage, and her life. The whitening is complete when differentiation is accomplished. Kristine now knew where she left off and Robert began. He was no longer all bad or all good; just as she took on human characteristics, so did he. Whether she loved him or not depended not so much on who he needed to be for her, nor on who she needed to be for him. Whether she loved him or not depended not so much on who he was when they married but who he was now. Kristine was able to see Robert in a more rounded way, and to have more reactions to him than merely grudging acquiescence, anger and love. She could be amused by him, or disappointed. She could feel compassion and arousal. Once she could feel all of these reactions she could also be involved with him again.

During the whitening, observation replaces separation. At the conclusion of the observation comes reunion.

> Robert, Tom and I are in a bath. Robert is at one end and Tom is between him and me. The water is a rich, dark green. Tom touches the inside of my thigh with a brush, and the intensity of the feeling takes my breath away. I try to hide my reaction from both of them, but cannot. Then, Tom is sitting on the side of the bath, shampooing his hair which is palish green. Robert tells me to move over so that Tom can get back in the bath, and rinse his hair. It is his bath anyway. I pull my legs in, and Tom returns to the bath, in the middle again. We feel sexually attracted, really in fun, but somehow I don't want Robert to know about it, although he seems to be promoting it.[2]

In a sense, the meaning of the dream is obvious. As if to light the way for bringing the passion and animation she has felt with Tom into her marriage with Robert, the dream supplies an image. She had seen her lack of passion as Robert's problem: "If he would only do such-and-such," Kristine had thought, "then I could love him." This dream said that she was in charge of her own passion and animation, that they belonged to her, which meant that her sexual feelings came from within her and were not dependent on the object, in this case Robert. It also meant that Tom had not activated her sexual feelings, but had been the projected embodiment of an inner animus which was accepting of and connected to her instinctive sexuality.

If a reunion is to take place in the marriage as well as intrapsychically, then instincts, aggression and sexuality have to be integrated, along with the need for relationship, as parts of the Self, and not solely as reactions to the partner. They have to be seen and accepted as Self-generated needs for gratification, as pro-active impulses *towards* the object, and not merely as reactions to it.

The dream unites the positive animus figure of Tom, who now symbolizes an accepting attitude toward the psychological reality of the instincts, with Robert, the objective husband. The pervasive green represents nature, the instinctive life. Robert is all for the integration of an accepting attitude towards sexual and relational instincts because the unconscious has intuitively picked up the objective reality of his desire to be involved with Kristine. Also objectively real was Kristine's fear of reunion, of jumping into the relationship with Robert again and of losing the distance that the "whitening" provided. This period is a time of detachment, of observation and understanding, but not of involvement.

Many marriages stop here, in the belief that less pain and more consciousness is the ultimate goal. As good as this may feel, it is a false conclusion because it is merely another equilibrium, another expression of knowledge distinct from passion. The equilibrium which preceded the blackening is the expression of the knowledge contained in the age-old wisdom of prevailing spirit. The knowledge of the prevailing spirit was a barrier to relating, an inhibiting force which oppressed large parts of our personality. The same danger exists in the whitening. Though a sense of enlightened security is attained, the body is yet to be involved. The goal is not only consciousness, but also passion.

With integration of the contents of this dream, Kristine found herself once again in love with Robert. It was by no means an infatuation: she was passionate because *she* was passionate. She was also substantially more conscious of herself and Robert than she had been when she first fell in love. She was conscious of how she saw her mother, her father, her own faults, and her own oppressive prevailing spirit in him, as well as how she had idealized expectations for him and herself which could not be lived out. She was, in effect, conscious of the psychological condition she was in when she first met Robert, which allowed her to realize how the individuation process alive within her brought her to the relationship, created Robert in her own unconscious image, pulled her away from him, and finally reunited her with her Self.

*   *   *   *   *   *

For his part, Robert had his own psychological separation arising out of Kristine's psychological work. Like so many spouses whose partners have erupted into psychological separation, Robert tried to put the lid back on. He argued, pleaded, cajoled, threatened, and bargained, though nothing worked. Kristine would not, perhaps even could not, put the lid back on. Robert had to make a decision. Either he would have to leave her or he would have to deal with her as she was. Like so many spouses, he tried to "make things right." He tried to find out what was wrong, what Kristine wanted from him. Of course she wanted nothing from him. She wanted to vent, to complain, and to accuse. Robert could make no sense of it as long as he focused on her, since he was not relating to her, but to his own perceived need to return the relationship to its former state of equilibrium. With Kristine uncooperative in this endeavor, Robert was literally stuck with himself.

All of Robert's attempts to reinstate the equilibrium created their own disequilibrium in the unconscious, which finally burst forth as a blackening, then a psychological separation of his own. With it came his own complaints, anger, resentment, disappointment, and so forth. Kristine now had to contend with him, and he now had the inner energy, released in the splitting of the anima, to fight it out with her. One of his dreams heralded the splitting of the anima and the beginning of his psychological separation. Like the dreams I presented in Chapter VI, the split image of the anima appears and separates Robert from Kristine, leading him to the shadow and to the prevailing spirit behind the equilibrium.

> Kristine and I are in Italy. We are trying to find a place to stay. We are sitting in a railway station and a man advises us where to stay. He is Swiss, and tells us the hotel is half demolished. I leave. I go alone. I go to a house where there is a girl outside. I ask something, and then another girl is there, a younger sister of the first girl. We go back to her house and when I see the older sister I say she should let me (alone) stay the night there. I am somehow implying that if she doesn't, I would make her sister run away with me. Then the father of these girls shows up, and he is accompanied by another guy who looks like an idiot.

Robert associated Italy with strong and uncontrolled emotions, and said that he and Kristine had spent a considerable amount of time there. Italy represents an attitude which generated tension in Robert because of the passions to which it was related. The tension is further indicated by the semidemolished building and the man who leads Robert to it, a Swiss who represents Robert's need for order and safety. Although Robert said that he did not like the Swiss, it is clear that his attempts to suppress Kristine's reactions are directed by this dream character. On the other hand, Robert liked the ease with which he thought the Italians could express themselves, and even felt some envy of this trait. From these associations it becomes clear that the relationship has ended up in Italy, the world of emotions activated by Kristine's revolt. Robert finds no psychic place to stay here because the territory is unfamiliar to him; that is, he is at a loss about what to do in the relationship. His initial reaction is to be the "Swiss," namely, rigid, safe, and orderly; but he finds that this place is already semidemolished. It is evident that he can no longer rely on those "Swiss" reactions which had helped him in the past. Now he is separated from his wife and goes to find a place for himself. He then encounters anima figures whom he associates with past relationships. It is clear that the power problem was present in these relationships.

The male ego attitude is to force the situation, to try to control events. The dream shows that as the anima image split, Robert's initial reaction is to try to control the constellated affects and contents. In concrete terms, Robert feels the need to withdraw from the relationship, to live out his sexual fantasies, and to suppress his anger. None of these reactions gives the anima figures of the dream a symbolic place in his life. By concretizing the fantasies and split in the anima image, Robert controls the situation and stays on top of it. The father of the girls represents his own father complex and his own patriarchal attitudes. The anima figures are therefore daughters of his patriarchal image.

The collective patriarchal image of woman has been projected onto real women, and creates a difficult situation in which women are expected to fulfill this image. The obvious problem is that women can never fulfill this image, and men and women alike suffer the consequences of the attempt. The situation, of course, may also be reversed, a woman trying to mold her husband into her idealized image of a man. In any event, the task for Robert is to separate the image of the feminine, the anima, from the reality of his wife. With the split of the anima image, he encounters both his anima and the father complex of which she is a product. He first confronts the prevailing spirit which controls his relationship to and image of the anima. As he approaches this problem, he is confronted by the "idiot," the son of the patriarchy, who represents the prejudices and rigidities of the prevailing spirit and the resulting behaviors. It is a common enough occurrence to see individuals acting in a kind of idiotic way as they produce their trite sayings and postures to rationalize away fundamental psychic facts. This showed up in Robert as trite rationalizations of his fundamental fear of himself and of a genuine relationship with Kristine. By confronting the father and the idiot, Robert would make some headway in changing his attitude toward himself and the feminine, and would then have a more flexible attitude with which to confront the other shadow parts of his personality, and which would have the effect of freeing his anima from her enchainment.

NOTES

1. In *The Psychology of Transference*, (*CW* 16) Jung writes:

> The painful conflict that begins with the *nigredo* or *tenebrositas* is described by the alchemists as the *separatio* or *divisio elementorum*, the *solutio, calcinatio, incineratio*, or as dismemberment of the body, atomization of the bridegroom in the body of the bride, and so on. While this extreme form of *disiunctio* is going on, there is a transformation of the arcanum—be it substance or spirit—which invariably turns out to be the mysterious Mercurius. In other words, out of the monstrous animal forms there gradually emerges a *res simplex*, whose nature is one and the same and yet consists of a duality. (pp. 197–198)

The *res simplex* is the elemental unity, the Anthropos who personifies both the Self and the individual free of collective identifications. The duality of which Jung speaks refers to the dual nature of Mercurius. As Mercurius Duplex, he is the psychic function connected to the dark world of the unconscious, yet he is at the same time the savior of the anima hidden in matter. In the *Mysterium Coniunctionis* Jung equates him with Eve: "The role [Eve] plays in regard to the princes of darkness corresponds to that of Mercurius duplex, who like her sets free the secret hidden in matter, the 'light above all lights', the *filius philosophorum*." (p. 41) Mercurius in thus connected to the spirit and to the world of the shadow and instincts; as we will see, he is also the spirit which frees the soul from its prison in matter, and at the same time the matter which enfolds the soul. Mercurius is also the feminine, and thus the soul imprisoned in the body. Jung writes:

> The "spirit" summoned from the dead is usually the spirit Mercurius, who, as the *anima mundi*, is inherent in all things in a latent state. (*Ibid.*, p. 238)

In the male, Mercurius takes the form of the feminine which must be freed from the chains of the body, while in the female he takes the form of the man who frees the

169

feminine from the grasp of the body. The images compensate the patriarchal collective ideal of the masculine, which denigrates the image and substances of the feminine. Differentiation has always been associated with the masculine psyche, to the extent that Neumann, in *The Origins and History of Consciousness,* contends that consciousness itself is masculine.

The Nazi slasher dream graphically illustrates the painfully repressive and wounding effects of identification with the patriarchal animus. In order for a woman to achieve psychic wholeness, this animus must at least temporarily be eliminated. The same problem also faces men. Although no corresponding collective image of "the woman a man should be" exists, a man who is one-sidedly masculine lives only a partial life. In the inner world, the patriarchal perspectives represented by the Nazi turn against instinct and receptivity, constantly creating doubts, guilt and fear. However, as with every psychic content, there is a reverse side to the problem. The discussion of Mercurius is necessary in order to understand the dream-figure of the soldier. The dual nature of Mercurius is represented by the knife and the telephone receiver.

The text accompanying Picture Seven (from the *Splendor Solis*) says that

> In order to receive the force that penetrates such subtle Matter, some alchemists calcinate Gold that they may dissolve it, and separate the elements until they reduce it to a volatile spirit or to the subtle nature of the greasy fumes of Mercury and Sulphur, and this then is the nearest matter, that combines most closely with gold, and receives the form of the occult Philosopher's Stone. (p. 22)

The knife represents the masculinity of Mercurius, the penetrating and differentiating aspect of the psyche, while the telephone receiver represents his feminine traits, the soul. The two have been joined together. The goal of the *separatio* is to separate or extract the soul (feeling) from the body (instincts) so that both may be experienced as essential spirit (see Picture Eight). The blood which flows from the womb of the woman represents not only the pain but also the transformation of the body into spirit. In the *Aurora Consurgens,* it is said:

> And when he baptizeth with blood, then he nourisheth, as it said: He gave me to drink of the saving water of wisdom, and again: his blood is drink indeed, for the seat of the soul is in the blood. (von Franz, *Aurora Consurgens,* p. 85)

Thus the blood represents the body-imprisoned soul which must be released from captivity. Another purpose of the *separatio* is to remove impure substances from the pure.

> Fifthly, he separateth the pure from the impure when he removeth all accidents from the soul, which are vapors, that is, evil odors, as is written: That fire separateth those things that are unlike and bringeth together those things that are like. (*Ibid.,* p. 93)

In the individual, the *separatio* is a violent and grisly period after which projections of shadow and anima or animus are removed from the spouse and the world. This process is clearly painful, since the partners must tear apart the body of their relationship in order to differentiate what belongs to them as individuals. The process, however, also serves the purpose of revitalizing or reanimating the relationship which had been dead up to now. The blood of the above dream represents the soul (feeling) released from the body (the end of repression) as well as the suffering of the individual during the *separatio.* In the Forty-Second Dictum of the *Turba Philosophorum* Ascanius says:

> Do ye not see that the complexion of a man is formed out of a soul and body; thus, also, must ye conjoin these, because the Philosophers, when they prepared the matters and

VII

conjoined spouses mutually in love with each other, behold there ascended from them a golden water. Stir up war between copper and quicksilver, until they go to destruction and are corrupted, because when the copper conceives the quicksilver it coagulates it, but when the quicksilver conceives the copper the copper is congealed into earth; stir up, therefore, a fight between them; destroy the body of the copper until it becomes a powder. But conjoin the male to the female, which are vapour and quicksilver. (*Turba Philosophorum,* ed. A. E. Waite, London: Robinson & Watkins, 1973, pp. 134–135)

The separation of the soul from the body and the removal of the impure from the pure release energies tied up in projection or repression. Since the Self cannot be repressed easily or for long, the energy of the contents repressed or not allowed to surface become negative and eventually overwhelm the ego and the collective ideals

VIII

with which it is identified. It is, however, of no value to become stuck in the instincts, just as it is of no value to be personally identified with the collective. In the *nigredo*, the unconscious overwhelmed the ego with negative fantasies, feelings and attitudes, which generated the *separatio*—which, like the *nigredo*, is a condition or state of being, not a one-time event.

2. By suffering tension and unbridled emotions, the old conscious attitude is softened, which makes room for the realization of a new spiritual attitude. The suffering may be described as the *mundificatio*, a stage of the alchemical process which the limbs are rejoined in the bath. Picture Nine—from the *Rosarium Philosophorum*—shows the merged image of the anima immersed in the bath, with clouds and rain above. The same idea is expressed in Picture Ten (from the *Splendor Solis*). In Jung's interpretation:

PHILOSOPHORVM

ABLVTIO VEL
Mundificatio

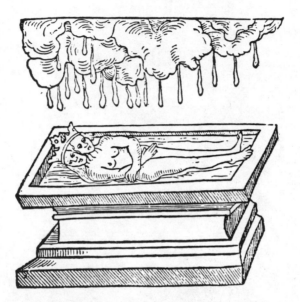

Hie felt der Tauw von himmel herab/
Vnnd wascht den schwarzen leyb im grab ab.

K iñ

IX

> The *mundificatio* (purification) means, as we have seen, the removal of the superfluities that always cling to merely natural products, and especially to the symbolic unconscious contents which the alchemist found projected into matter. This is what the laboratory worker called the *extractio animae,* and what in the psychological field we would call the working through of the idea contained in the dream. (*CW* 16, pp. 277–278)

The purification brings a new light out of the darkness of the *nigredo,* and reunites the limbs separated in the *separatio.* As we have already seen, positive animus images are connected to the chthonic world, which compensates the conscious spiritual attitude. This same chthonic image is represented in the dreams of men by the whore, the dark older woman, the helpful peasant woman, etc. Jung says of the chthonic image:

> The unconscious is the spirit of chthonic nature and contains the archetypal images of the *Sapientia Dei.* But the intellect of modern civilized man has strayed too far in the world

X

of consciousness, so that it received a violent shock when it suddenly beheld the face of
its mother, the earth. (*Ibid.*, p. 272)

This passage indicates the connection between the chthonic images of the dreams
already presented and the instinctual world of nature and the unconscious. In the
separatio, the feminine is released from bondage in the body and connected to the new
spiritual attitude represented by the positive animus of a woman, or a positive shadow
figure in a man.

However, the contrasexual image is still split until the purification takes place. At
that point the negative and positive images are reunited as the psyche begins to
reintegrate its separated contents. The black contents are thus transformed by the bath
and reunited with the positive contents carried by the positive contrasexual image. This

bath dream represents the possibility of a reunion between the dreamer's positive and negative animus images. Robert represents the body which has been torn apart in the *separatio,* because it is onto him that all the instinctive and shadow contents have been projected. He is, however, also the old prevailing spirit which was joined to the body in the *nigredo.* That is, the ego withdrew from its old collective identifications, but projected the blame onto the spouse, who carried the responsibility for having repressed and suppressed the dreamer. In this way the spouse became the target of aggression. Tom represents the positive image of the animus, a continued evolution of the inner masculine spirit. It becomes clear at the end of the dream that Robert is promoting the union between the dreamer and Tom, because it is through this union that he will be purified of the darkness projected onto him. As well as a symbol of the reunited contrasexual images, the *mundificatio* is "an attempt to discriminate the mixture, to sort out the *coincidenta oppositorium* in which the individual has been caught." (*Ibid.,* p. 293)

By symbolically reuniting with the positive animus image, the dreamer can finally see what belongs essentially to her, and she then can withdraw those projections which have darkened her spouse. It is no wonder that Robert, in the dream, is promoting the union. According to Jung,

> The process of differentiating the ego from the unconscious, then, has its equivalent in the *mundificatio,* and, just as this is the necessary condition for the return of the soul to the body, so the body is necessary if the unconscious is not to have destructive effects on the ego-consciousness, for it is the body that gives bounds to the personality. (*Ibid.,* p. 294)

Since the spouse is so intimately connected in the infatuation with anima or animus and the shadow as well as the instincts, he in effect "becomes" the unconscious *per se.* Through the *separatio* and its after-effects, shadow contents are integrated. In this way the dreamer becomes the alchemist's soul extracted from the body—Robert, or the unconscious.

However, a further task is the reunification of the soul (the dreamer) and essential spirit (Tom) with the body (Robert). Conscious and unconscious become partners, and at the same time connect essential spirit and soul to the instincts. Without the instincts, the body (the individual) has no limitations and is not fixed. It is through the instincts that one knows what belongs to and what is a violation of one's Self. In this sense, one's animal or wild nature becomes an integral part of one's psychic functioning, and it is the purification which makes this possible. The same idea is expressed in other dreams.

> Fritz and I are being chased by a wild man, and we run out onto a wharf on the ocean. We run to its end but are unable to get to the secret pathway which leads from the wharf to an island. The wild man is going to grab us, and in a measure of heroism, Fritz catches him and plunges into the water. I can see Fritz in the water, and the wild man has jumped in also. Fritz and the wild man get out of the water. The wild man now looks young and healthy. He looks up and says, with a profound look of religious awe on his face, that he has been changed in the waters, he is a new man having been plunged into the depths and left for dead. He is now happy to have believed himself dead since through that he was transformed.

The wild man obviously represents a more primitive, instinctual part of the dreamer killed in the *nigredo.* The body is dismembered in the *separatio* and given life in the *mundificatio.* The cleansing or purification process makes the dark light—the dark contents become light, that is, conscious, and expand the possibilities available to the conscious personality. This is the *albedo* of the alchemists, the whitening, which was frequently mistaken for the goal of the work. In the *Mysterium Coniunctionis*, Jung calls the *albedo* the *unio mentalis* because it is the union of the spirit with the soul. The purification process cleanses the dark contents, but if the body is not rejoined to the soul and spirit, the process is incomplete.

> It is significant for the whole of alchemy that in Dorn's view a mental union was not the culminating point but merely the first stage of the procedure. The second stage is reached when the mental union, that is, the unity of spirit and soul, is conjoined with the body. But a consummation of the *mysterium coniunctionis* can be expected only when the unity of spirit, soul, and body is made one with the original *unus mundus*. (*Mysterium Coniunctionis*, p. 465)

The seductive quality of the *unio mentalis* lies in the fact that one has overcome the tension of the internal opposites. Spirit and soul are at peace with one another. After the turbulence and suffering of the *nigredo* and *separatio*, the *albedo* feels like the end. There is no great tension between the psychic forces which had been at odds with one another.

In a marriage the *albedo* takes the form of knowledge and consciousness of what is happening between the partners and within one's self. There is, however, a certain distance between the partners, borne of the desire to retain the objectivity of the *unio mentalis*. If a concrete separation has taken place, one has a relatively objective view of one's own role, as well as the role of the spouse, in creating the marriage and separation. However, what is still missing is the body, the instincts and the relationship. That is, there is an inner sense of meaning in the *albedo*, but real relationship is still lacking. This can only come as the body is joined to the spirit and soul. The *unio mentalis* is an intellectual state in which a new conscious viewpoint and attitude has been wed to a new relationship to the feeling and psychic contents of our personalities. However, if this cannot be translated into a new way of functioning in the world and with a partner, an autistic quality to the relationship develops. Still lacking is the transformation of one's self and the transformation of the world around one. It is this process which Jung has called the *unus mundus*, the transformation of inner experiences and the expression and experience of this transformation in the world.

It is, however, important to emphasize that the *mysterium coniunctionis* is an inner *and* an outer experience. The meaning of the *coniunctio* is not "a fusion of the individual with his environment, or even his adaptation to it, but a *unio mystica* with the potential world." (*Ibid.*, p. 537) The importance of this statement lies in the fact that the *coniunctio* brings into being a state in which the personality is returned to the beginning. That is, in marriage the potentialities of the world of relationship stand before the couple, and the marriage potentially contains all the possible ways two people can relate to one another. The marriage then becomes container for the expression of the individual personalities of the partners.

CHAPTER VIII

CONCLUSION: THE SYMBOLIC LIFE

Every author must struggle, after the manuscript is complete, to decide on that perfect title which both captures the reader's imagination and says what he wants to say about his message. Over the course of the years it took me to write this book, literally hundreds of titles floated through my imagination, some of them having to do with animation, others of them about rekindling lost love. I played with them all, letting them hang above me like a kite, to see how they flew, and whether any would stay aloft beyond the merest fraction of the time it has taken me to finish the book. One of those titles stayed with me longer than most, only to be discarded because its humor carried a bit of the prejudice which the reader will undoubtedly have come to recognize. The title was: *People Who Love People, and The People Who Love Them.* The title is, of course, a take-off on a currently popular genre of work that has to do with men who hate women, and the women who love them, women who make bad choices, men who are afraid to love, women who have a Cinderella complex, and so forth. It is not surprising that hundreds of thousands if not millions of people read these books as quickly as they leave the presses. I suppose that we could infer that the readers of these books hunger for good non-fiction and have only objective reasons for digesting their contents as ravenously as they do. But that doesn't seem likely to me. I may be wrong; however, it seems more likely that the readers of these books identify with the problems described in them, and are looking for solutions to them. A number of

177

people in my groups have read one or more of these books, hoping to find some answers. They, like millions of others, have painful problems they want solved.

I prefer not to infer that all these millions of people have something pathologically wrong with them, and what struck me as so satisfying about my original title was the possibility of conveying that the problems we encounter in relationships are inherent to them. That is the point of my book. Whether it is a problem of bad choices born of an underdeveloped psychological perspective and a lack of differentiation in the midst of intrapsychic conflict; or the problem of a man who hates women and the woman who loves him, or the problem of a woman whose Cinderella self-image confines her to scrubbing the floors while those around her have a ball; whether it is any number of other problems described and analyzed and resolved in these popular books, they all have one central connecting link. They are all about a *psyche coming into being in the conscious world*. They are all about extending the limits of the known world, within us and around us.

I would prefer to see the perspectives in this book as differentiated and objective and empirical. Yet I won't argue with anyone who calls it prejudice when I claim that my dissatisfaction with popular relationship books comes from the literal and concrete interpretations of the psychological problems they describe. The judgment in the titles of these books, about men who "hate," women who love "too much," women who make "bad" choices, pathologizes the unconscious. Such judgments make people out to be "sick," or at least "wrong." What I have tried to do is to re-imagine the problems of relationship, to see them not in context of what is adapted and expected, not from the perspective of a narrow prevailing spirit, but from the perspective of what is in the nature of being human. If this approach is not taken, then the man who hates is no more than a static cardboard cut-out, with no other faces than the "woman who loves him." What is truly important is what brings them together and keeps them together even after they have been told that they are bad for each other.

If we can see that the problems of marriage and separation are an extension and expression of a psyche coming into being in the conscious world, then we are intensely engaged in the most fundamental work of life: the individuation process. And those with whom we have the most disconcerting encounters, whether of infatuation or conflict, take on symbolic value as outer expressions of inner characters, some of whom we cannot tolerate, others whom we wish to become, and others with whom we wish to unite. The symbolic life, seeing the outer world and inner world as mirror reflections of one another, is the consequence, the end product, the goal of the work of individuation. It is not a goal which is ever attained, but an ongoing process of understanding that we are behind and within the experiences we encounter and go after, *i.e. as in ♭* and that those who move us with joy and pain are within us as well as around us. *I've got you under my skin...*

The symbolic life is not attained by sitting on a mountain or contemplating the nature of the universe, but in everyday relationships and interactions with the people and the world around us. It is in the infatuation, equilibrium, blackening, separation, whitening and reunion that what is unconscious in us moves through the layers of psychological resistance and identification, to a consciousness which can understand with the head, integrate with the heart, and live out with the instincts what is innately human in us. In the end, the joys and pains of life no longer say something only about the world out there, beyond us, but more to the point, about what is in us and makes itself known through pain and joy.

This book is not, however, a call to inaction in the outer world, or to a naive acceptance of the behaviors in our fellow human beings that violate our laws and the boundaries of human decency. Consciousness should not be confused with inactive acceptance. The woman who is beaten and accepts it is conscious neither of the damage done her by her mate nor of the inner prevailing spirit which has enslaved her spirit and her instinct. The abused woman must just as surely see her husband for what he is as she must see her inaction as her enchainment. She is not off the hook when she sees the inner enchainment of the prevailing spirit, but changes nothing and continues to be beaten. Nor is she off the hook if she takes the actions necessary to protect herself, but makes no effort to understand the inner and outer conditions which made her tolerate the abuse. *+ # abuse too ?*

The individuation process demands no less than the struggle to attain the wisdom to see within as well as without, to see the mirror images of ourselves in the world, and the world's mirror image within us. And in the struggle to attain the wisdom of the symbolic life, we begin to create myth—for solutions to the inner and outer conflicts are just that, the myths of our lives. Each time a conflict is resolved, when the infatuation to reunion circuit is completed, a new piece of the myth is fitted into place. We have one more bit of information about who we are, why we are here, and what we are to do in and with our lives.

The myth created in us is no illusion, no collective image or embodiment of a prevailing spirit which robs us of our uniqueness. If we can place the pains and joys of relationship in context of a symbolic life and mythologem, we can see the stages in the circuit as symbolic

?? See The Power of Myth by Joseph Campbell; book + video BL 304 J 674 1988 v. 1 in Olson Lib.

representations of what is coming to the surface within us: the infatuation, the animation which threatens our assumptions and functions in
the world; the equilibrium, a temporary respite of security to prepare
for or avoid the looming battle; the blackening, the inevitable end to
peace in our world, the world pressing in on us to find and integrate
the new way shown in the infatuation; the separation, the creation of
the distance to see what has welled up from; the whitening, the image,
what we are capable of; the reunion, the life in the world with what we
have come to become.

The myth we create out of the individuation process and its circuit
from infatuation to reunion is no illusion, because it is not only the
expression of the volatile world of prevailing spirit, which may change
with the direction of the wind; it is also the expression of essential
spirit, which places us immediately in our life and experiences, and the
instincts which ground us in our humanity, show us our limitations,
and connect us with the world around us.

x   i.e. as in "get real"

BIBLIOGRAPHY

Edinger, Edward F. "Psychology and Alchemy. I: Introduction. II: Calcinatio." In *Quadrant,* 11, 1, Summer 1978

———. "Psychology and Alchemy. III: Solutio." In *Quadrant,* 11, 2, Winter 1978

———. "Psychology and Alchemy. VI: Mortificatio." In *Quadrant,* 14, 1, Spring 1981

———. "Psychology and Alchemy. VII: Separatio." In *Quadrant,* 14, 2, Fall 1981

———. "Psychology and Alchemy. VIII: Coniunctio." In *Quadrant,* 15, 1, Spring 1982

Ellenberger, H. *The Discovery of the Unconscious.* New York: Basic Books, 1970

Foerster, Werner. *A Selection of Gnostic Texts, Vol. 1: Patristic Evidence.* Oxford: Oxford University Press, 1972

———. *A Selection of Gnostic Texts, Vol. 2: Coptic and Mandaic Sources.* Oxford: Oxford University Press, 1974

Fromm, Erich. *The Art of Loving.* New York: Bantam Books, 1967

Guggenbuhl-Craig, Adolf. *Marriage: Dead or Alive.* Murray Stein, tr. Zurich: Spring Publications, 1977

Janik, A., and S. Toulmin. *Wittgenstein's Vienna.* New York: Simon & Schuster (A Touchstone Book), 1973

Jonas, Hans. *The Gnostic Religion: The Message of the Alien God and the Beginnings of Christianity.* 2nd Ed. Boston: Beacon Press, 1963

Jung, C.G. *The Collected Works of C.G. Jung,* Vols. 1–20. R.F.C. Hull, tr.

William McGuire *et al.*, Eds. Bollingen Series XX. Princeton: Princeton University Press, 1954–1980

Kerényi, Karl. *The Heroes of the Greeks*. Southampton: Thames & Hudson, 1978

Mattoon, Mary Ann. *Jungian Psychology in Perspective*. New York: Free Press, 1981

————. *Understanding Dreams*. Dallas: Spring Publications, 1984

Medawar, P.B. *The Limits of Science*. New York: Harper & Row, 1984

Neumann, Erich. *The Origins and History of Consciousness*. R.F.C. Hull, tr. Bollingen Series XLII. Princeton: Princeton University Press, 1954

The New English Bible. London: Oxford University Press, Cambridge University Press, 1970

Paracelsus, A.P.T.B. *The Hermetic and Alchemical Writings of Paracelsus*. A.E. Waite, Ed. Berkeley: Shambhala Publications, 1976

Patai, Raphael. *The Hebrew Goddess*. New York: Avon Books, 1978

Philatelus, Eugenius. *The Works of Thomas Vaughan*. A.E. Waite, Ed. London: Theosophical Publishing House, 1919

Read, John. *Prelude to Chemistry: An Outline of Alchemy, Its Literature and Relationships*. London: G. Bell & Sons, Ltd., 1936

Scholem, Gershem, G. *Kabbalah*. New York: Quadrangle Press, 1974. *On Kabbalah and its Symbolism*. London: Routledge & Kegan Paul, 1965

Trismosin, Solomon. *Splendor Solis*. London: Kegan, Trench, Trubner & Co., Ltd, N.D.

Von Franz, Marie-Louise. *Aurora Consurgens*. London: Routledge & Kegan Paul, 1966

Waite, A.E. *The Hermetic Museum*, Vol. 1. York Beach, ME: Samuel Weiser, Inc., (in press)

————. *Turbas Philosophorum Or Assembly of the Sages*. London: Robinson & Watkins, 1973

INDEX

SIGO PRESS

SIGO PRESS publishes books in psychology
which continue the work of C.G. Jung, the great
Swiss psychoanalyst and founder of analytical
psychology. Each season SIGO brings out a small
but distinctive list of titles intended to make a
lasting contribution to psychology and human
thought. These books are invaluable reading for
Jungians, psychologists, students and scholars
and provide enrichment and insight to general
readers as well. In the Jungian Classics Series,
well-known Jungian works are brought back into
print in popular editions.

Among the SIGO
books now in print
are books on

Psychology
Healing
Religion
Women's Studies
Alchemy
Dreams
Bodywork
Child Abuse
Astrology & Metaphysics
Mythology
Sandplay Therapy
Death & Dying

For a free catalog, write to

SIGO PRESS
25 New Chardon Street, #8748B
Boston, Massachusetts, 02114

1/16/98 ... ± p. 149

I ask is there love or only...
infatuation followed by all
this shit? This book analyzes
love to death!
or only "fairly tolerable relationships"?
What ever happened to "I love you
just because...!" Porque gosto! Porque sí!

      Given my sollipsitic bent, see p. 179 top ½
this analysis makes love out to
be an exercise in self-deception
+ delusion which leaves one w/
the prospect that, for example,
arranged marriages have more or
as much of a chance to succeed
as so called romantic ones;
like buying a suit off the rack,
but such a conclusion is too
discouraging. Why bother?! But
wait, see ch. VIII, p. 177-80.

Other Titles from Sigo Press

The Unholy Bible *by June Singer*
$32.00 cloth, $15.95 paper

Emotional Child Abuse *by Joel Covitz*
$24.95 cloth, $13.95 paper

Dreams of a Woman *by Shelia Moon*
$27.50 cloth, $13.95 paper

Androgyny *by June Singer*
$24.95 cloth, $14.95 paper

The Dream-The Vision of the Night *by Max Zeller*
$21.95 cloth, $14.95 paper

Sandplay Studies *by Bradway et al.*
$35.00 cloth, $18.95 paper

Symbols Come Alive in the Sand *by Evelyn Dundas*
$27.50 cloth, $14.95 paper

Inner World of Childhood *by Frances G. Wickes*
$27.50 cloth, $14.95 paper

Inner World of Man *by Frances G. Wickes*
$27.50 cloth, $14.95 paper

Inner World of Choice *by Frances G. Wickes*
$27.50 cloth, $14.95 paper

Available from SIGO PRESS, 25 New Chardon Street, #8748A, Boston, Massachusetts, 02114. tel. (508) 526-7064

In England: Element Books, Ltd., Longmead, Shaftesbury, Dorset, SP7 8PL. tel. (0747) 51339, Shaftesbury.